Essay Writing Police:

On Guard of Your Literacy

Tracing errors, misprints and mishaps students make

By EssayShark

Copyright Page

Table of Contents

Acknowledgments Page **4**

Introduction **5**

Chapter 1. Essay Structure Mistakes **6**

    1.1. Essay Introduction Mistakes 7

    1.2. Mistakes to Avoid in the Main Body 12

    1.3. Mistakes to Avoid in the Conclusion 20

Chapter 2. Essay Format Mistakes **24**

    2.1. Mistakes to Avoid in APA Format 25

    2.2. Mistakes to Avoid in MLA Format 36

    2.3. Mistakes to Avoid in Chicago Format 43

    2.4. Mistakes to Avoid in Turabian Format 51

Chapter 3. Main Grammatical Mistakes in Essay Writing **59**

Chapter 4. Stylistic Mistakes in Academic Writing **73**

    4.1. Word Choice 74

    4.2. Commonly Confused Words 78

    4.3. Style 87

    4.4. Sentence Structure 91

Chapter 5. Mistakes in Following Essay Structure and Requirements **96**

    5.1. Compare and Contrast 96

    5.2. Argumentative 98

    5.3. Narrative 100

    5.4. Critical 101

    5.5 Definition 102

Chapter 6. Plagiarism Mistakes – Quoting, Citing, Paraphrasing **105**

Final Thoughts **114**

Acknowledgments Page

Our team is proud to introduce our new book. The launch would not have happened without the perseverance and effort of all members of our publishing team, which includes writers, editors, designers, and other experts whose names you can see below. Due to the high qualification, personal involvement, and experience of all members of our team, you are able to use such a useful book for your studies. Every person whose name is listed below deserves great acknowledgment. Thanks to their close and efficient collaboration, one more book from EssayShark has been released. Meet the team:

Project editor: Derek Lynch

Guides author: Polina Nefedova

Publisher: Matthew Wright

Production editor: Drake Parker

Focus group: Jillian Sanders, Alison Murphy, Jakob Rogers, Brooke Woods, Mark Cooper

Cover page: Kylie Butler

Proofreader: Trenton Campbell

Editorial assistant: Wyatt Cox

Concept by: Tyler Collins

Introduction

All written works contain mistakes. Even if you take a book released by an authoritative publisher, you will probably find at least one mistake after a thorough search. Unfortunately, making mistakes is part of human nature and you can't fight it. However, you can develop your literacy so that it is almost impeccable. In *Essay Writing Police: On Guard of Your Literacy*, we have gathered a list of the most common mistakes students make and presented the ways to avoid and correct them.

Our book doesn't focus only on one type of lapse. You will be able to get acquainted with information about structural, stylistic, grammatical, and formatting mistakes: their descriptions, analysis, the ways to correct them, and the explanation on how to avoid them. Each case is supported with examples. Also, you will find out how to avoid plagiarism, which is crucial in academic writing. Reading *Essay Writing Police: On Guard of Your Literacy* will not guarantee all your papers to be free of mistakes. However, we will give you clues on what errors to look for and how to correct them. Start your thorny path to outstanding academic achievement with us!

Chapter 1. Essay Structure Mistakes

An essay consists of ideas, arguments, and facts which must be composed in a logical way to increase impact on readers. A successfully written narration requires proper structuring, similar to a mathematical formula in which the result depends on the constituents you choose. Moreover, the order of presented data pieces is vital to place your claims in the relevant essay parts for the audience to perceive the information in the most efficient way.

The three main parts of an essay (introduction, main body, conclusion) have peculiarities and structural standards to follow and, as a consequence, you may receive a lower grade for the evaluation even though you may have outstanding content and perfect formatting. In Chapter 1, we have summarized primary mistakes students make while structuring essays. Here, you may find the most common introduction, main body, and conclusion errors to analyze and avoid in your further works. Each chapter includes several mistakes which are discussed in detail. We have identified them, and provided you with examples for each of the mistakes as well as recommendations on how to avoid such. In order to make the information more visually perceptive, we have included tables. In addition, each chapter part illustrates two examples for each mistake as incorrect and correct versions for you to notice the difference and understand the main idea of the explanation.

The advice provided will help you to notice distinctive structural features of each essay part and make ideas flow as one complex, meaningful unit. Please, refer to the information mentioned in Chapter 1 to organize your essay and fit all the requirements related to structure. We hope you will find our guide interesting and recommendations useful!

1.1. Essay Introduction Mistakes

The introductory part of an essay is vital. It makes the first impression on the reader, who may either read it till the end or consider it as a waste of time. A catchy introduction should include the contextual background of the work, which will lead the audience to the strong and convincing thesis statement. In order to make the essay introduction "hooky" and impressive, the top five mistakes to avoid will be defined.

Mistake #1. Irrelevant introduction.

One of the most common errors in writing an introductory section relates to generalizing the information mentioned without narrowing it to the particular topic ("Essay Introduction"). Students usually think that starting the essay with the general information is the key to success, but making it too broad without focusing on the concept regarded further in the essay is a sure way to fail.

Incorrect: *The topic of feminism has been an important and quite disputable issue discussed in many countries.*

The mentioned example is an obvious statement, making the sentence sweeping enough not to attract the attention of the reader. In order to avoid this mistake, you should distinguish the primary focus of the essay and narrow the opening sentence to the point of the further enlightened arguments ("Essay Introduction"). The first part of the introduction has to lead the audience to the thesis sentence offering a limited context.

Correct: *The topic of feminism is one of the most discussed issues in the USA due to the strengthened position of women in society after the Second Word War.*

Mistake #2. Introduction structure.

Introduction Structure

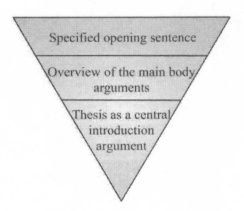

A successful introduction equals a well-structured introduction. While writing the introduction to the essay, students often do not pay much attention to its structure as they suppose it has to consist of randomly taken parts of the essay. Nevertheless, the introduction has to be organized according to the essay's construction of the arguments.

Incorrect: *Vikings, also known as the Norsemen from Scandinavia, are well known for their sea navigation skills and raids. One of the well-documented raids by the Vikings was their incursion in England. Their raids and settlement in England made a huge impact on English culture and civilization, especially on its language.*

The primary problem in the example is a general lack of information about the arguments which will be introduced further in the essay. In order to avoid this mistake, you should define which data is covered in each paragraph and enlighten their central elements in the introduction.

Correct: *Vikings, also known as the Norsemen from Scandinavia, are well-known for their sea navigation skills and raids. The incursion in England provoked the spread of Viking settlements which impacted the transformation of the language. The raids in England expanded the vocabulary, changing the word structure by adding suffixes and endings which may be defined in modern language.*

Mistake #3. Absence of a thesis.

A thesis statement is the central argument of the introduction which ties all elements together. The absence of a thesis is a widespread mistake, and will destroy the structure. Neglecting this part of the introduction leads to doubts on your actual contribution to understanding the topic ("Developing a Thesis Statement").

Incorrect: *Constant usage of the Internet among youngsters is the problem provoking addiction and mental degradation. Young generations spend most of their time visiting web pages, watching different videos, and communicating with each other in the digital world more often than in real life.*

In the example mentioned, the final remark of the introductory part should make the reader interested in the topic and understand the intentions of the writer from one sentence. The idea is that you should develop the thesis, choosing several ideas from the main body part, and show the reader what solution to the problem to expect.

Correct: *Constant usage of the Internet among youngsters is the problem provoking addiction and mental degradation. Young generations spend most of the time visiting web pages, watching diverse videos, and communicating with each other in the digital world more often than in real life. In order to change the current situation of youth degradation, parents have to take charge of the Internet utilization and implement restrictions on the overwhelming usage of social networks.*

9

Mistake #4. Unclear thesis.

Another common mistake is having a poorly composed thesis. The error often deals with the lack of the main argument and the inability to explain why it should be "argued and defended" (Rosenwasser and Stephen 79). Furthermore, a weak thesis statement may include a claim based on personal opinion, which makes the introduction subjective rather than objective (82).

Incorrect: *I agree that the home delivery service in the US is beneficial for businesses as it offers companies the opportunity to spread the product efficiently and gain more profits.*

In order to avoid this mistake, you should keep aside your attitude towards the question regarded and concentrate on proving the issues with arguments. As well, consider the outcomes of the paper and enhance your thesis with the results to be gained at the end of the essay.

*Personal attitude remarks are forbidden in all of the possible essay types EXCEPT personal reflection, response, and narrative essays.

Correct: *The aim of the following paper is to define the perspective of the home delivery service trend in the US and analyze the benefits of its implementation by businesses.*

Mistake #5. Introduction beginning with a thesis.

A thesis is the conclusion of the first part of the essay which answers the questions asked and closes previously discussed analysis steps (Andreatta 87). Placing a thesis before the arguments and analysis is a common mistake, as it ruins the aim of having the introduction provide the conclusion before the pieces of evidence (88).

Incorrect: *Further implementation of the technologies requires employees to enhance their skills and develop the knowledge in order to become competitive. The utilization of the automotive machines during the production stage increases the rate of unemployment among the population. Artificial intelligence substitutes human labor, eradicating most of the professions, leaving people without work or an earning option in particular.*

When choosing the thesis statement, REMEMBER to place it at the end of the introduction to follow the structure and make it complete the whole picture.

10

Correct: *The utilization of automated machines during the production stage increases the rate of unemployment among the population. Artificial intelligence substitutes human labor, eradicating most of the professions, leaving people without work or earning options in particular. Further implementation of the technologies requires employees to enhance their skills and develop the knowledge in order to become competitive.*

The introductory part of an essay reflects the essentiality of the topic discussed, and making it well-structured is an opportunity to attract the attention of your readers and make them follow your ideas. Avoiding the mistakes mentioned above is the chance to illustrate that you are confident in the stated and can easily confirm it with further arguments. Good luck!

Works Cited

Andreatta, Britt. *Navigating the Research University*. 3rd ed. New York, N.Y. Wadsworth Publishing, 2009. Print.

"Developing a Thesis Statement." *CSTW – Center for the Study and Teaching of Writing*. Web.12 July 2017.

"Essay Introduction." *Owll.massey.ac.nz*. Web. Accessed 12 July 2017.

Rosenwasser, David, and Jill Stephen. *Writing Analytically*. 2nd ed. Harcourt College Publishers, 2000.Print.

1.2. Mistakes to Avoid in the Main Body

The main body of an essay is the foundation of the whole narration, as it contains statements and arguments to fulfill the ideas discussed in the introduction. In order to make the main body precise and well-structured, a list has been developed of the five most common mistakes to avoid.

Mistake #1. Paragraph division.

Most students do not pay much attention to the paragraph division while writing an essay ("Avoiding Common Mistakes in Essay Structure"). They start writing, forgetting about what was mentioned before and the structure becomes not essential enough. Furthermore, many writers consider word count as the most important issue, dividing each paragraph into an equal amount of words to make the essay look perfect.

Incorrect: *Henry Ford used to have great interest in inventions, and his desire was so intense that he left his studies at school, left his farm, and even refused an inheritance. All this was done in order to work in Thomas Edison's factory. After work, at night in his garage, Henry worked on the creation of their car. In 1986 he finished his first work, which culminated in an analog of the ATV, which utilized gasoline (Pinedo). Henry's neighbors were terrified when he first started his vehicle and drove it in the street. The success in the*

12

construction of the first machines prompted Ford to join the company that produces cars, as he needed money. He was engaged in automobile construction. The success in the construction of the first machines prompted Ford to join the company that produced cars, as he needed money. The directors of the company were interested in producing certain vehicle models, so they were not excited about the inventions of a young implementer. For this reason, Henry's cooperation with the company was revoked. In the first ten years of the twentieth century, more than five hundred companies dealing with car manufacturing were founded, though only a few of them were developed. During this period of time, Ford also created his first business, but unfortunately, it collapsed after one year of existence.

Irish roots allowed Ford to accept the first defeat in the business exclusively as a kind of training, and he continued his attempts to create automobile production. As a result, the Ford Motor Company appeared in 1903, which has since reached worldwide success (Bak, 2003). He introduced the world's first assembly line in the production of automobiles.

In the presented essay, the writer divided the text into two paragraphs, despite the word count requiring at least three. As well, the first paragraph is almost four times bigger than the second. In order to avoid this mistake, think of several ideas which you would like to enlighten and support and ensure that the parts of the body are almost equal. The point is that you should pay attention to the word count, although some paragraphs may be one or two sentences longer.

Correct: *Henry Ford used to have a great interest in inventions, and his desire was so intense that he left his studies at school, left his farm, and even refused an inheritance. All this was done in order to work in Thomas Edison's factory. After work, at night in his garage, Henry worked on the creation of their car. In 1986 he finished his first work, which culminated in an analog of the ATV, which utilized gasoline (Pinedo). The success in the construction of the first machines prompted Ford to join a company that produced cars, as he needed money. He was engaged in automobile construction. The directors of the company were interested in producing certain vehicle models, so they were not excited about the* *inventions of a young implementer. For this reason, Henry's cooperation with the company was revoked.*

Ford's Irish roots allowed him to accept the first defeat in the business exclusively as a kind of training, and he continued his attempts to create for automobile production. As a result, the Ford Motor Company appeared in 1903, which has since reached worldwide success (Bak, 2003). Ford's idea was to produce a machine that a factory worker could afford, which meant it could not have a high price. It became the parent image of the American Dream, suggesting his employees to dream of their own car. Ford simplified the construction of the car and standardized its parts and mechanisms. Thus, he introduced the world's first assembly line in the production of automobiles. This innovative solution immediately moved his company to become industry leaders, leaving his competitors far behind.

Companies tend to face different operational risks, and Ford is not an exception. Since the company executes supply management, operational risks are high. Representatives of the Ford Motor Company use the TTR (Time-To-Recover) model in order to identify the conceivable risk of suppliers. Strategically, the company compares the risk exposure of suppliers and other information concerning the total amount of expenses in order to generate strategies referred to different types of suppliers. Ford is interested in identifying suppliers whose disruption impact is sensitive to the given TTR information.

Mistake #2. Shortened paragraphs.

The second most widespread mistake concerns shortened paragraphs. The normal section should be at least four well-constructed sentences long. Remember that a couple of sentences do not form a paragraph. The paragraph has to include ideas and arguments to fulfill the stated information, which is nearly impossible to cover in two sentences ("5 Main Mistakes in Writing a Paragraph").

Incorrect: *One of the earliest theories regarding why people want to be liked was given by Karen Horney in her book Self Analysis (1950). Her theory of neurosis stated that when a person is exposed to anxiety, he or she employs several defense mechanisms to overcome the fear.*

The illustrated section consists of only two sentences, and without including a central idea or supporting arguments. You should decide which claim to mention, and frame it with pieces of evidence in the form of two to three complex sentences containing accomplished arguments.

Correct: *One of the earliest theories regarding why people want to be liked was given by Karen Horney in her book Self Analysis (1950). Her theory of neurosis stated that when a person is exposed to anxiety, he or she employs several defense mechanisms to overcome the fear. However, when the defense mechanisms are used too often, such an apparent form of behavior is known as neurotic. It may also be characterized with needs for prestige, power, and affection.*

Mistake #3. Too lengthy paragraphs.

Having paragraphs that are too lengthy is common in essays, as the reader may miss the point and be lost in thousands of unnecessary words. The problem of having sections that are too long creates a high probability of the reader losing focus ("5 Main Mistakes in Writing a Paragraph"). In addition, the reading process may become boring.

Incorrect: *With time, the understanding of the appropriate age to move out has changed. In previous years, it was associated with marriage and certain educational conditions, but the situation has become quite different. The social conditions always play an initial role in the process of the development of the personality. But modern society now has the reverse views on morals and permit people to make their own decisions. Hartley underlines that nowadays the decision about the appropriate age for this step belongs only to the family and the economical possibilities of its members, and does not depend on the community. The* tendency to stay in the parental house longer than the previous generations has been a recent trend. In the article, Hartley (1993) mentioned:

"The respondents were 138 young adults interviewed at age 23; they had also been interviewed seven years previously when they were aged 16. At the time of the second interview, 27 percent of the women and 49 percent of the men were living with parents. These figures are consistent with estimated national figures for 23-year-olds living with parents in 1993 (that is, 25 percent of women and 44 percent of men)."

The author claims that the process of leaving plays the initial role in the life of the young adult and the most appropriate age to this step is 23 years. This approach, according to the article, has more advantages than disadvantages in the process of personal development.

The writer obfuscates the point of the paragraph as the initial idea is difficult to determine. To make the size of each section relevant, try to make it four to six sentences long to make each claim complete and interesting to perceive.

Correct: With time, the understanding of the appropriate age to move out has changed. The social conditions always play an initial role in the process of the development of the personality, although the views are quite different now. Hartley underlines that nowadays the decision about the appropriate age for this step belongs only to the family and the economical possibilities of its members, and does not depend on the community. The tendency to stay in the parental house longer than in previous generations has been a recent trend. In the article, Hartley (1993) mentioned:

"The respondents were 138 young adults interviewed at age 23; they had also been interviewed seven years previously when they were aged 16. At the time of the second interview, 27 percent of the women and 49 percent of the men were living with parents.

These figures are consistent with estimated national figures for 23-year-olds living with parents in 1993 (that is, 25 percent of women and 44 percent of men)."

The author claims that the process of leaving plays an initial role in the life of a young adult which becomes a vital stage of personal development.

Mistake #4. Absence of a topic sentence.

The lack of a topic sentence is a common mistake among students, as they usually start the paragraph with an argument rather than telling the reader of the idea the paragraph is about to follow (Schmitz 316). The topic sentence is similar to the thesis statement, which has to lead the audience to the points discussed later ("5 Main Mistakes in Writing a Paragraph").

Incorrect: *First of all, scientists doubt that the ideology justifies the use of medical technology and, thus, eliminates the use of alternative practices and procedures. Due to the fact that a reaction in infectious diseases is a characteristic of the 19th century, it does not meet the needs of modern society. Modern community, partly because of the aging population, is in need of health systems that can respond to chronic diseases. Other scientists claim that it is not appropriate for the treatment of mental illness and correcting deviant behavior. Treatment can be more effective if we consider the patient as a person having social and psychological needs.*

You should concentrate on the narrowed topic and arguments of each paragraph and write one introductory sentence covering the main idea to be discussed. Remember that the topic sentence helps you to stay focused on the particular issue, eliminating the possibility to make a step aside and strictly follow the concept regarded.

Correct: *It is important to mention the significant number of controversies and oppositional opinions circling around the theory and the ideology it covers. First of all, scientists doubt that the ideology justifies the use of medical technology and, thus, eliminates the use of alternative practices and procedures. Due to the fact that a reaction in infectious diseases is a characteristic of the 19th century, it does not meet the needs of modern society. Modern* *community, partly because of the aging population, is in need of health systems that can respond to chronic diseases. Other scientists claim that it is not appropriate for the treatment of mental illness and for correcting deviant behavior. Treatment can be more effective if we consider the patient as a person having social and psychological needs.*

Mistake #5. Lack of arguments and supporting sentences.

Most essay paragraphs tend to include many sophisticated words, but they do not make any sense and are written only to match the word count required. The structure of a section is often collapsed as students consider it unnecessary. Nevertheless, the lack of arguments as supportive sentences may lead to the chaotic collection of statements without enhancing the idea.

Incorrect: *It is not a secret that psychiatrists and psychotherapists have distinct approaches and methods to treating illness. Unlike a psychiatrist, a therapist will carefully ask depressed patients about their recent troubles, crucial losses, or childhood trauma. The therapist will ask the patient the associated questions, so that the doctor may confirm the previous assumptions made. If the patient perceives the understanding of the causes as insight, he or she will remove the anxiety about the depression and perceive it as entirely appropriate. As a consequence, the patient will be able to effect self-control.*

The example shows that the absence of supporting sentences does not make the claim confirmed as it should be. In order to avoid such a mistake, think of or search for the pieces of evidence appropriate for the idea and write two or three additional arguments to strengthen the opinion. Historical facts, specific examples, and in-text citations from academic sources may be useful to elaborate upon your ideas (Milgram).

Correct: *It is not a secret that psychiatrists and psychotherapists have distinct approaches and methods to treating illness. Unlike a psychiatrist, a therapist will carefully ask depressed patients about their recent troubles, crucial losses, or childhood trauma. The therapist believes that the patient experiences severe mental distress because of painful experiences from childhood — for example, because of parents who divorced or gave less*

18

love than what was required for the child. The therapist will ask the patient the associated questions, and if the client recalls something related to it, the doctor will be convinced in the previous assumptions made. If the patient perceives the understanding of the cause as insight, he will remove his anxiety about the depression, perceive it as entirely appropriate, but, on the other hand, in the future will control emotions in a more patient manner.

Take into account that not only the essay in general but its every unit requires proper structure. Each well-constructed paragraph in the main body illustrates your ability to prove ideas. Avoid the most common mistakes presented above to make the writing process easy and the result of your work persuasive and interesting. Good luck!

Works Cited

"Avoiding Common Mistakes in Essay Structure." *Write.com*, 2017, http://www.write.com/writing-guides/assignment-writing/writing-process/avoiding-common-mistakes-in-essay-structure/.

"5 Main Mistakes in Writing a Paragraph." *4Writers.net*, 2017, https://4writers.net/blog/5-main-mistakes-in-writing-a-paragraph/.

Milgram, Jack. "How to Avoid Common Mistakes in Essay Writing." *Custom-Writing.org*, 2017, https://custom-writing.org/blog/writing-tips/free-essay-writing-tips/26841.html.

Andy, Schmitz. *Successful Writing*. 1st ed., https://2012Books.Lardbucket.org/, 2012.

1.3. Mistakes to Avoid in the Conclusion

The conclusion is the final note of an essay which the reader may keep in mind much longer than any of the stated arguments or examples. Notwithstanding, students often make mistakes in this part which decreases the impact on the audience and the overall chances to get the highest grade. In the following guide, we are going to discuss common mistakes in conclusions and give you recommendations on how to avoid them.

Mistake #1. Failing to restate the thesis statement.

Thesis statement mentioned in introduction: *The impact of the leader's inspirational and motivational speeches for employees appears to have a short-term effect and requires additional approaches to be utilized as a developed bonus system and a range of career opportunities.*

Conclusion

Incorrect: *To conclude, employees are defined to feel inspiration shortly after a leader's speeches, although the method may be useful in combination with bonuses and career opportunities developed by the company.*

The mistake in this part concerns the lack of a restated thesis which was written earlier in the introductory section. You need to pick up the initial idea presented in the thesis statement and illustrate it from the perspective of your understanding of the outcomes gained after the research. Here, you should not just change the word order of the introduction thesis, but echo its sense with your reflection on the topic.

Correct: *To conclude, leaders often make speeches to make employees more motivated; however, the approach is not the winning one. As well, inspirational words are likely to increase the overall working capacity. The impact of the leader's inspirational and motivational speeches for employees appears to have a short-term effect and requires additional approaches to be utilized as a developed bonus system and a range of career opportunities.*

Mistake #2. No difference between introductory and concluding parts.

Students often have difficulties with identifying the difference between the introduction and conclusion, and make them structurally similar ("6 Most Common Mistakes in Essay Writing"). Nevertheless, you should remember that each part has its own peculiarities to follow.

Note! You may read more about common mistakes in introductions earlier in the guide.

Incorrect:

Introduction	Conclusion
The theme of slavery has been quite disputable in recent years due to the high percentage of African Americans living in the U.S. Racism, as one of the starting points leading to slavery, may be regarded as a phenomenon still occurring in modern society. The purpose of the following paper is to research the development of racism through American history and the impact it provides on Americans using a quantitative research method.	*To conclude, the topic of slavery is essential in the U.S. due to the historical events which occurred within its territory. Past times have significantly influenced modern American society members and their attitude toward African Americans. Despite widespread opinion that racism left American borders along with slavery, it still exists.*

The primary mistake of the concluding part demonstrated above concerns its structure and ideas. You may notice that the conclusion is similar to the introduction and does not provide the reader with research results. As well, the thesis statement is not appropriately restated, as it should be placed first in the conclusion. Please, refer to the table demonstrated below to notice the main differentiating points in the conclusion and introduction to avoid structural mistakes.

Differences Between Introduction and Conclusion

Introduction	Conclusion
1. Specified opening sentence. (Avoid overly generalized information. Be specific.) 2. Review of the arguments presented in the main body. 3. Central argument enlightened in the introduction (i.e. Thesis Statement).	1. Restated thesis statement regarding initial concept of the essay. 2. Short summary of arguments and facts illustrated in main body. 3. Concluding remarks to reiterate essay theme ("Writing Guide: Introduction and Conclusion").

Correct:

Introduction	Conclusion
The theme of slavery has been quite disputable in recent years due to the high percentage of African Americans living in the U.S. Racism, as one of the starting points leading to slavery, may be regarded as a phenomenon still occurring in modern society. The purpose of the following paper is to research the development of racism through American history and the impact it provides	*To conclude, the research maintained has illustrated that the phenomenon of racism has been developing for hundreds of years and has significantly influenced Americans and their views. The quantitative study proved that the majority of white Americans do not regard African Americans as a lower social class, although a minor part does. The problem requires further research on its potential solutions to decrease social*

on Americans using a quantitative research method.	*contradictions.*

Mistake #3. Citations and new information.

One of the most widespread mistakes is to add new information in the conclusion. The point is that this part of an essay does not bring any data pieces which are not explained in the main body. Please, be attentive and write about facts already discussed.

One more crucial mistake students make refers to citations in conclusions. Remember that citations make sense in the main body as a supportive tool for arguments enlightened. There is no need to insert other people's opinions in the place where you should conclude your own.

In this guide, we have discussed the most common mistakes students make in conclusions and provided you with recommendations on how to avoid them. Please, pay attention to the points illustrated above and ensure your essay is free of such errors. Good luck!

Works Cited

"6 Most Common Mistakes in Essay Writing." *HBCU Lifestyle*, 2017.

   https://hbculifestyle.com/common-essay-writing-mistakes/.

"Writing Guide: Introduction and Conclusion." *Usu.edu*,

   2017.https://www.usu.edu/markdamen/WritingGuide/24intro.htm.

"Writing Essays for Dummies." May, 2017. https://essayshark.com/blog/writing-essays-for-

   dummies/

Chapter 2. Essay Format Mistakes

Format style is a vital part of the writing process as, primarily, it illustrates your ability to follow instructions. Each style has specifications and is utilized according to the research field. Academic essays may be formatted in one of the four main styles (APA, MLA, Chicago, Turabian) corresponding to a particular research field. A set of standards has been developed to make students more disciplined while writing narrations and consistent in organizing ideas. Moreover, while composing essays students often insert citations to support arguments, and their incorrect citations may lead to plagiarism.

In the following chapter, we have discussed four main format types. All styles have similar general guidelines, such as with font, margins, and spacing, although other formatting points vary. In each guide, we showed you which data should be included on the title page, which of the four formats require a running head, and how a reference list should be organized. We have utilized tables with the same literature for each format for you to notice the nuances of reference formatting for diverse styles. In addition, Turabian and Chicago formatting styles diversify from APA and MLA with the utilization of footnotes which are enlightened in the guide. In-text citations are vital while writing an essay and we uncovered all the distinctions of their proper formatting as well.

Regarding the following guide, you will realize that formats are not challenging anymore, and being acquainted with recommendations provided will ensure your assignments are completed accordingly. Dealing with APA, MLA, Chicago, or Turabian styles will become an easy and pleasant procedure and will make you adhere to following a set of standards and be able to pursue established instructions.

2.1. Mistakes to Avoid in APA Format

Correct formatting is the key to making your essay within the style requirements. APA (American Psychological Association) style is widely spread while writing articles based on social science resources. In case your professor asks you to follow APA style, pay attention to the main mistakes made by students to avoid them and get the highest grade possible for formatting.

Mistake #1. General guidelines.

Errors in following the initial guidelines of APA style is the most common mistake among students. The style requires accurate margins, font, spacing, and indents to be utilized. Please have a look at the example below.

Incorrect:

CHILD'S HAPPINESS   2

Abstract

Modern society has changed child's vision of happiness. With the development of IT, kids have been under the impact of the technologies which convert their minds and the perception of what childhood is about. Internet access, accounts on social networks, and time-consuming online games are the reality which children face. As well, the desires have transformed along with the permissibility measures. All the factors mentioned veil the meaning of true child happiness which are to be managed by parents.

Keywords: child's happiness, social obstacles, parental education

The example illustrates all the possible mistakes while following APA style general guidelines. You may see double margins along with Arial 14 pt font. Moreover, the font is gray but not black. The text is 1.5 spaced. In order to avoid the mistakes mentioned, please take the following points into account:

- One-inch margin format on all sides.

- The text should be double spaced.

- Recommended APA font is Times New Roman 12 pt.

- Clear font (black).

Correct:

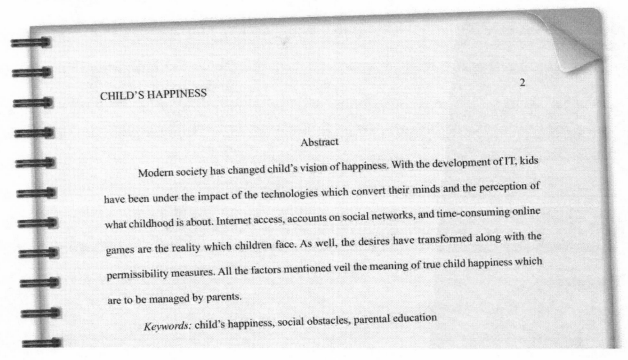

CHILD'S HAPPINESS

Abstract

Modern society has changed child's vision of happiness. With the development of IT, kids have been under the impact of the technologies which convert their minds and the perception of what childhood is about. Internet access, accounts on social networks, and time-consuming online games are the reality which children face. As well, the desires have transformed along with the permissibility measures. All the factors mentioned veil the meaning of true child happiness which are to be managed by parents.

Keywords: child's happiness, social obstacles, parental education

Mistake #2. Abstract page.

An abstract page is a separate part of the essay which has to be formatted according to APA style specifications.

Incorrect:

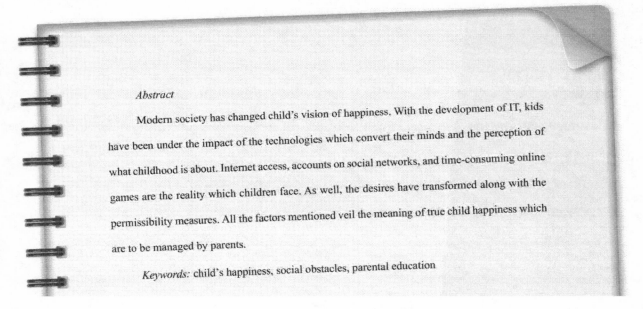

Abstract

Modern society has changed child's vision of happiness. With the development of IT, kids have been under the impact of the technologies which convert their minds and the perception of what childhood is about. Internet access, accounts on social networks, and time-consuming online games are the reality which children face. As well, the desires have transformed along with the permissibility measures. All the factors mentioned veil the meaning of true child happiness which are to be managed by parents.

Keywords: child's happiness, social obstacles, parental education

The mentioned example includes indent, page header, and "Abstract" mistakes. In order to avoid the errors make sure that the abstract is placed on a separate page after the title page. The page header (capitalized) should be included as well as the page number. Remember that the word "Abstract" has to be centered and without formatting, quotation marks, underlining, or italics. In case you place keywords at the end of the abstract, you should indent it italicizing the word "Keywords" ("Purdue OWL: APA Formatting and Style Guide").

Remember that an abstract should fit within 250 words ("Purdue OWL: APA Formatting and Style Guide").

Correct:

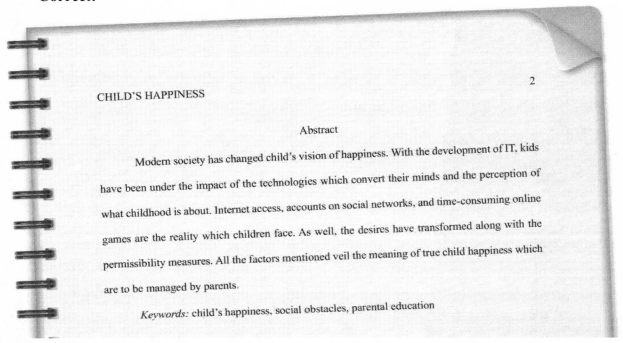

Mistake #3. Running head.

Running head is the shortened version of the essay title which should include the main idea of the article ("APA Formatting Rules for Your Paper"). The running head is one more area containing widespread mistakes while writing an essay. Most students follow the wrong formatting or simply forget to mention the running head throughout the essay.

Incorrect:

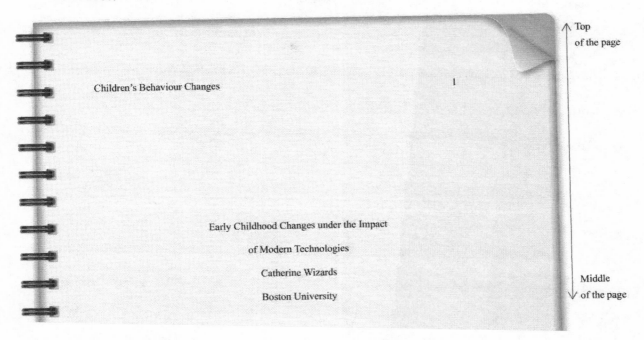

The mistake enlightened above concerns the lack of the word "Running Head" on the title page. The header should be capitalized. Further in the essay, there is no need to use it but the header itself.

Correct:

Mistake #4. Title page.

The title page is the first impression of the essay. The title itself captures the attention of a reader and has to be precise with no abbreviations or senseless words and phrases ("APA Formatting Rules for Your Paper"). The title has to be one or two lines long as well.

Incorrect:

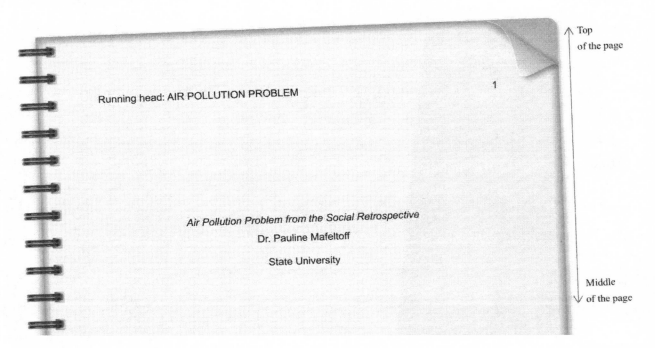

In the example mentioned above, the student violates the rules of proper APA style formatting. The text has to be centered, double-spaced, Times New Roman 12 pt font, with no other text changes. Moreover, the format forbids using any possible author's titles as Mr. or Dr. ("APA Formatting Rules for Your Paper"). The structure has to be the following:

- Title.

- Author's name.

- Affiliation.

Correct:

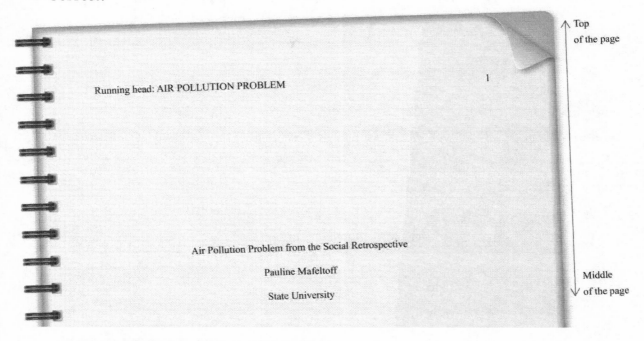

Mistake #5. References and in-text citations.

The list of references is often confusing for students as it may seem difficult to remember all the APA style requirements. Nevertheless, to make the process of referencing the sources less stressful, please look at the table below to ensure that your sources are referenced and cited correctly ("APA 6th Examples").

Journal Articles

Reference Type	Referenced Source	In-Text Citation
Electronic journal article (including DOI)	Strinic, V. (2015). Arguments in Support and Against Euthanasia. *British Journal of Medicine and Medical Research, 9* (7), 1-12. http://dx.doi.org/10.9734/bjmmr/2015/19151	(Strinic, 2015)
Printed article	Samah, I., Rashid, I., Rani, M., Rahman, N., Ali, M., & Abdullah, M. (2015). The roles of price perception and physical environment in determining customer loyalty: evidence from fast food restaurant of	(Samah et al., 2015)

	Malaysia. *International Journal of Development Research, 5*(5), 4366-4370.	

Books

Reference Type	Referenced Source	In-Text Citation
1 author	Chittister, J. (2013). *Happiness* (1st ed., pp. 34-37). Grand Rapids: Wm. B. Eerdmans Publishing Co.	(Chittister, 2013)
2 authors	Weber, M., & Henderson, A. (2012). *Max Weber* (2nd ed., pp. 56-61). Mansfield Centre, CT: Martino Publishing.	(Weber & Henderson, 2012)
3-7 authors	Oxlade, C., Farrow, A., Miller, A., & Dharmapala, V. (2013). *Modern Medicine* (1st ed., pp. 91-106). Chicago, Ill.: Raintree.	(Oxlade et al., 2013)
8 or more authors	Bourn, D., Andreotti, V., Asbrand, B., Hicks, D., Laycock, A., & Leonard, A. et al. (2012). *Development Education* (1st ed., pp. 6-10). London: Institute of Education Press.	(Bourn et al., 2012)
Chapter of an edited book	Hatten, T. (2016). Small Business Finance. In *Small Business Management: Entrepreneurship and Beyond* (6th ed., pp. 220-245). Boston, USA: Cengage Learning.	(Hatten, 2016)

Online Sources

Reference Type	Referenced Source	In-Text Citation
Webpage	Ramos, A. (2015). *Chile's President responds to girl's*	(Ramos, 2015)

	dramatic plea. CNN. Retrieved 11 May 2017, from http://edition.cnn.com/2015/03/01/americas/chile-girl-euthanasia-request/	
Video	*The Psychology of Self-Motivation	Scott Geller	TEDxVirginiaTech.* (2013). https://www.youtube.com/watch?v=7sxpKhIbr0E	(The Psychology of Self-Motivation | Scott Geller | TEDxVirginia Tech, 2013)
Blog	Nieh, K. (2017, August 2017). Starting Your First Job Search on LinkedIn [Web blog post]. Retrieved from https://blog.linkedin.com/2017/august/17/starting-your-first-job-search-on-linkedin	(Nieh, 2017)

* While formatting the sources make sure that the word "References" is centered, all the resources are in alphabetic order, double-spaced, and with 1-inch margins.

Mistake #7. Tables and figures.

Tables and figures are the essential part of an essay in APA as they provide the reader with visual information which is easy to comprehend. Nevertheless, incorrect citing and titling may lead to a grade decrease, and even plagiarism.

Incorrect example of a table title: *Correlation between music and language*

Here, the author does not mention the table number, which may lead the reader to confusion. Moreover, the reader may be lost in the diversity of tables inserted into the essay. As well, the text should not be capitalized or italicized.

Correct example of a table title: Table 1. Correlation between music and language

Figures have to be titled as well as the tables. Figures and tables taken from scholarly sources are to be referenced according to the basic APA style format.

Remember that while citing sources beneath figures or tables, you do not need to double reference them in the reference list at the end of your essay.

Incorrect
Interrelation between society and personal perception of happiness. Reprinted from Happiness (p 24), by A. White, 2017, New York, US. Balington. Copyright (2017) by Austen White.

The example above shows that the writer does not mention the figure number. Moreover, the italics should be used not for the figure title but the resource title. At the end of the borrowed figure, the permission for copying has to be included.

Note that you should follow the same steps while citing a copied table.

Correct
Figure 1. Interrelation between society and personal perception of happiness. Reprinted from *Happiness* (p 24), by A. White, 2017, New York, US. Balington. Copyright (2017) by Austen White. Reprinted with permission.

APA style requires proper attention to the formatting nuances which are enlightened in the guide above. Use them and get the highest grade for your essay.

Works Cited

"APA 6th Examples." University of Canterbury.

http://library.canterbury.ac.nz/files/APA_6th_guide.pdf.

"APA Formatting Rules for Your Paper." *Easybib Blog*, 2017.

http://www.easybib.com/guides/students/writing-guide/iv-write/a-formatting/apa-paper-

formatting/.

Angeli, Elizabeth, et al. "APA Formatting and Style Guide." *The Purdue Owl*. Purdue U Writing

Lab, 13 May, 2016. https://owl.english.purdue.edu/owl/resource/560/01/.

2.2. Mistakes to Avoid in MLA Format

MLA (Modern Language Association) style is usually utilized to write essays on humanities and liberal arts. While creating an essay based on MLA style you should focus your attention on several basic principles to ensure the essay is accurately formatted.

Mistake #1. General guidelines.

Mistakes in the general guidelines are widely committed by students, although MLA style does not require significant efforts to format your paper correctly. There are several primary principles you should remember about general guidelines in MLA style (Russell et al. "MLA Formatting and Style Guide"):

- Times New Roman font, 12 pt is obligatory.

- 1-inch margins on all sides.

- Double-spaced text.

- Black font.

Notice that each style (APA, MLA, Chicago, Harvard) has the same general requirements as mentioned above. You may see the mistakes in the following general guidelines earlier in the chapter about the most common mistakes in APA style.

Please keep in mind that abstracts are used in APA style only, and if you see that an abstract is needed, check the format requirements once again.

Mistake #2. Running head.

One of the most common mistakes while following MLA style deals with a missing running head, or its incorrect implementation. The point is that students often put the title of the paper as a Running Head, though it is not correct. Please look at the example below.

Incorrect:

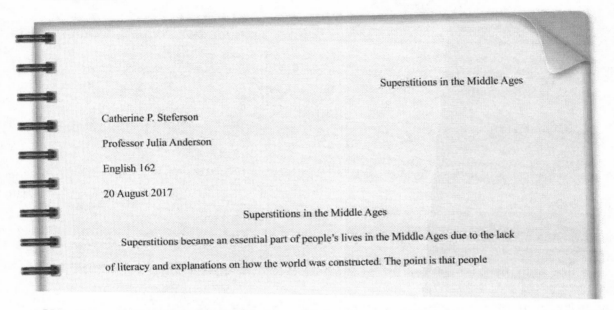

You may see that the author of the essay incorrectly wrote the title in the running head, and instead should have mentioned her last name and the page number after it.

Correct:

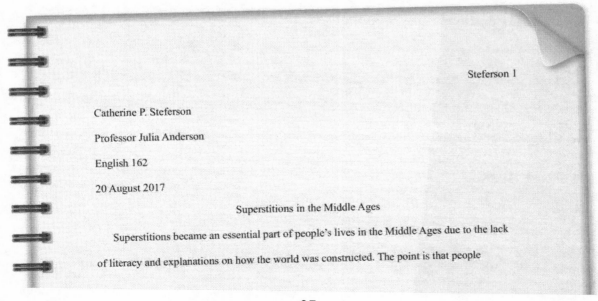

* Moreover, further in the essay you need to follow the same running head, which includes your last name only and the page number.

Mistake #3. Title page.

Often, students provide a separate title page for the essay, although MLA style does not require it. Don't make the title page as a separate page, mentioning much more data than she had to. In MLA style there are a few main data pieces only to cover (Russell, et al. "MLA Formatting and Style Guide"):

- Your first and last name.

- Professor's name.

- Course number.

- Date (day, month, year).

* Make note of the fact that you do not need to capitalize or italicize the information listed above or do any other actions to change the text.

You should place the data on the left of the page without indents made. Moreover, the title of the essay has to follow basic information on the left. The title is to be centered with no highlighting, underlining, or bold font. Ensure that in the title all the words start with a capital letter except prepositions, articles, and conjunctions (Russell, et. al. "MLA Formatting and Style Guide").

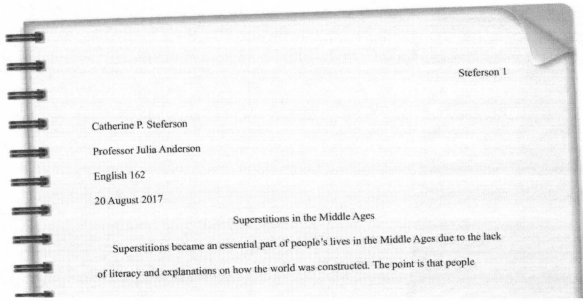

Mistake #4. Works Cited page and in-text citations.

MLA Works Cited pages require a separate page at the end of the essay. The words "Works Cited" have to be centered using Times New Roman font 12 pt, and not being capitalized, highlighted, underlined, or italicized. In order to ensure your sources are formatted correctly, please follow the table on how to reference and cite diverse resources mentioned below.

Journal Articles

Reference Type	Referenced Source	In-Text Citation
Electronic journal article (including DOI)	Strinic, Visnja. "Arguments in Support and Against Euthanasia." *British Journal of Medicine and Medical Research*, vol 9, no. 7, 2015, pp. 1-12. *Sciencedomain International*, doi:10.9734/bjmmr/2015/19151.	(Strinic 5)
Printed article	Samah, Irza Hanie Abu et al. "The Roles of Price Perception and Physical Environment in Determining Customer Loyalty: Evidence from Fast Food Restaurant of Malaysia.." *International Journal of Development Research*, vol 5, no. 5, 2015, pp. 4366-4370.	(Samah, Irza Hanie Abu et al. 4367)

Books

Reference Type	Referenced Source	In-Text Citation
1 author	Chittister, Joan. *Happiness*. 1st ed., Grand Rapids, Wm. B. Eerdmans Publishing Co., 2013.	(Chittister 46)
2 authors	Weber, Max, and Anketell Matthew Henderson. *Max Weber*. 2nd ed., Mansfield Centre, CT, Martino Publishing, 2012.	(Weber, Max, and Anketell Matthew Henderson 68)

3-7 authors	Oxlade, Chris et al. *Modern Medicine*. 1st ed., Chicago, Ill., Raintree, 2013.	(Oxlade, Chris et al. 182)
8 or more authors	Bourn, Douglas et al. *Development Education*. 1st ed., London, Institute Of Education Press, 2012.	(Bourn et al. 201)
Chapter of an edited book	Hatten, Timothy S. "Small Business Finance." *Small Business Management: Entrepreneurship and Beyond*, 6th ed., Cengage Learning, Boston, USA, 2016, pp. 220-245.	(Hatten 232)

Online Sources

Reference Type	Referenced Source	In-Text Citation
Webpage	Ramos, Annie. "Chile's President Responds to Girl's Dramatic Plea – CNN." *CNN*, 2015, http://edition.cnn.com/2015/03/01/americas/chile-girl-euthanasia-request/.	(Ramos)
Video	"The Psychology of Self-Motivation	Scott Geller	TedxVirginiaTech." https://www.youtube.com/watch?V=7Sxpkhibr0e, 2013.	(The Psychology of Self-Motivation | Scott Geller | TEDxVirginiaTech)
Blog	Nieh, Kylan. "Starting Your First Job Search on LinkedIn." *LinkedIn Official Blog*, 2017, https://blog.linkedin.com/2017/august/17/starting-your-first-job-search-on-linkedin.	(Nieh)

You may compare the sources referenced above with the ones mentioned in the chapter on APA Style.

Mistake #5. Tables and figures.

The most common mistake related to the usage of tables and figures is their incorrect naming and citing. In case you fail to properly reference the source from which you got the table or figure, you may be accused of being academically dishonest. Please take into account the examples illustrated below to avoid the mistakes.

Incorrect Example of a Table Title
Table 1: Correlation between music and language From: Molley, Peter. "Music and Language as Interconnected Notions." *Alabama Journal of Linguistic Sciences,* vol. 5, no. 10, 2014, pp. 10-38. ***(A table taken from a source)***

The example shows the incorrect naming of a table as there should not be a colon after the word "Table." Furthermore, the table title has to be placed on the new line after "Table 1." The resource from which the table was taken has to appear after the table and the word "Source."

Correct Example of a Table Title
Table 1 Correlation between music and language ***(A table taken from a source)*** Source: Molley, Peter. "Music and Language as Interconnected Notions." *Alabama Journal of Linguistic Sciences,* vol. 5, no. 10, 2014, pp. 10-38.

Figures in MLA style are titled in a particular manner. Here, students often make format mistakes which lead to a grade decrease.

*Remember that while citing figures or tables, you do not need to reference the sources again in the Works Cited list at the end of your essay.

Incorrect
Figure 1. *Interrelation between society and personal perception of happiness*: White, Andrew. *Happiness.* 1st ed*.,* New York, US. Balington, 26 October 2017, p. 24.

The example above shows that the writer does not follow the basics of MLA style. The word "Figure" has to be shortened to "**Fig.**" and bold font must be used. The name of the table should not be italicized and should be followed by the word "from" with a colon after it ("Libguides: MLA Citation Guide (8th Edition): Images, Charts, Graphs, Maps & Tables"). Next, fill in the referenced source formatted according to MLA style requirements.

Correct
Fig. 1. Interrelation between society and personal perception of happiness from: White, Andrew. *Happiness.* 1st ed*.,* New York, US. Balington, 26 October 2017, p. 24.

MLA style differs from other formats and requires particular attention to details. Follow our guide on how to avoid the mistakes connected to MLA style to ensure your essay fits all the requirements. Good luck!

Works Cited

"Libguides: MLA Citation Guide (8th Edition): Images, Charts, Graphs, Maps & Tables." *Columbiacollege-Ca.Libguides.com*, 2017. https://columbiacollege-ca.libguides.com/mla/images.

Russel, Tony, et. al. "MLA Formatting and Style Guide." *The Purdue Owl*. Purdue U Writing Lab, 5 Sept. 2017. https://owl.english.purdue.edu/owl/resource/747/01/.

2.3. Mistakes to Avoid in Chicago Format

The Chicago Notes and Bibliography (NB) system is commonly used while writing essays on humanities usually on economics and history. The following style differs from others with the usage of footnotes instead of citations. In order to make the essay fit all the elements required in Chicago NB style, understand the primary mistakes made by students to avoid them in your essay.

Mistake #1. General guidelines.

Following general guidelines is often a weak place while writing an essay, as most often students forget about such details as correct font or margin utilization. Please regard the information on the basic requirements to general guidelines to ensure your essay satisfies the claims:

- Times New Roman font, 12 pt.

- 1-inch margins on all sides.

- Double-spaced text.

- Black font.

Pay attention that each style (APA, MLA, Chicago, Harvard) has the same general guideline requirements as mentioned above. You may see the mistakes in the following general guidelines earlier in the chapter about the most common mistakes of APA style.

Mistake #2. Running head.

While formatting the essay according to Chicago NB style, students often repeat the same mistake with the running head. REMEMBER that Chicago NB Style is minimalistic and does not require a running head at all. The only issue to mention is the page number at the right upper corner. Look at the example below.

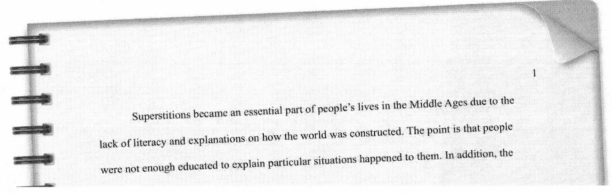

Mistake #3. Title page.

The title page in Chicago NB style has to be formatted correctly, as it may impact the grade you will get on the paper. The common mistake in this section belongs to the wrong data order and incorrect formatting of the essay title.

The essay title has to be capitalized. The structure has to be the following:

- First name, last name.

- Class data.

- Date (month, day, year).

Thirdly, name and class information has to be formatted with single margins.

Pay attention to the fact that single margins in Chicago NB style are used for block quotations, figures, and table titles only (Clements, et al. "Chicago Manual of Style 16th Edition"). *The rest of the text has to be double-spaced.*

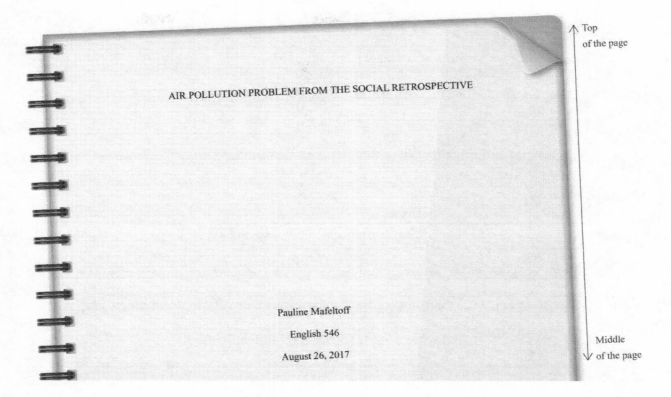

Mistake #4. Bibliography.

Chicago NB style differentiates itself from other styles in the bibliography, as the list of sources has to be formatted in a specific manner. The primary requirement is to start the reference list from a new page at the end of your essay. Here, you should use the word "Bibliography" instead of "Works Cited" or "References." Be attentive while following the table below on how to reference various types of sources in Chicago NB style.

Journal Articles

Reference Type	Referenced Source
Electronic journal article (including DOI)	Strinic, Visnja. 2015. "Arguments in Support and Against Euthanasia." *British Journal of Medicine and Medical Research* 9 (7): 1-12. doi:10.9734/bjmmr/2015/19151.
Printed article	Samah, Irza Hanie Abu, Intan Maizura Abd Rashid, Mohd Juraij Abd Rani, Nor Irwani Abdul Rahman, Muhammad Ahmar Ali, and Muhammad Fazlee Sham Abdullah. 2017. "The Roles of Price Perception and

	Physical Environment in Determining Customer Loyalty: Evidence from Fast Food Restaurant of Malaysia." *International Journal of Development Research* 5 (5): 4366-4370.

Books

Reference Type	Referenced Source
1 author	Chittister, Joan. 2013. *Happiness*. 1st ed. Grand Rapids: Wm. B. Eerdmans Publishing Co.
2 authors	Weber, Max, and Anketell Matthew Henderson. 2012. *Max Weber*. 2nd ed. Mansfield Centre, CT: Martino Publishing.
3-7 authors	Oxlade, Chris, Andrew Farrow, Adam Miller, and Vaarunika Dharmapala. 2013. *Modern Medicine*. 1st ed. Chicago, Ill.: Raintree.
8 or more authors	Bourn, Douglas, Vanessa Andreotti, Barbara Asbrand, David Hicks, Anna Luise Laycock, Alison Leonard, Annette Scheunpflug, and Gillian Temple. 2012. *Development Education*. London: Institute of Education Press.
Chapter of an edited book	Hatten, Timothy S. 2016. "Small Business Finance." In *Small Business Management: Entrepreneurship and Beyond*, 6th ed., 220-245. Boston, USA: Cengage Learning.

Online Sources

Reference Type	Referenced Source
Webpage	Ramos, Annie. 2015. "Chile's President Responds to Girl's Dramatic Plea – CNN." *CNN*. http://edition.cnn.com/2015/03/01/americas/chile-girl-euthanasia-request/.
Video	*The Psychology of Self-Motivation	Scott Geller	Tedxvirginiatech*. 2013.

	Video. https://www.youtube.com/watch?V=7Sxpkhibr0e.
Blog	Nieh, Kylan. 2017. "Starting Your First Job Search on LinkedIn." Blog. https://Blog.Linkedin.Com/2017/August/17/Starting-Your-First-Job-Search-On-Linkedin.

* You may compare the sources referenced above with the ones mentioned in the chapters on APA and MLA Styles.

Mistake #5. Footnotes.

The distinctive feature of the Chicago NB style refers to the utilization of footnotes, or endnotes, throughout an essay. A footnote includes the referenced source which will appear later in the bibliography list. Here, you should not insert citations in brackets as you need to in MLA or APA Styles. The common mistake related to Chicago footnotes relates to the constant repeat of the full titles of sources being used more than once.

Here is an example of a source footnoted for the first time in the essay:

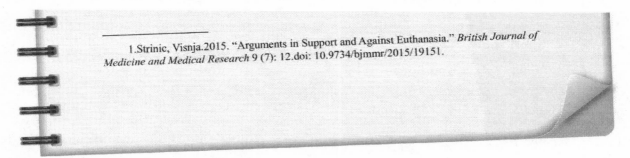

In case the resource is about to be used as a subsequent note citation, the title should be shortened. Have a look at the next example.

In case you use a source often throughout your essay, you should mention the abbreviation "Ibid." (which means "in the same place"), put a comma after it and the page from where you got the information (Clements, et al. "Chicago Manual of Style 16th Edition").

The issues you need to keep in mind while formatting footnotes ("Library Guides: Citing and Referencing: Chicago"):

- The first line of a footnote has to be intended.

- An extra line space between the footnotes.

- Use "Ibid., (page number)" in case you use the same source often throughout your essay.

Tip: In case you are confused with how to insert a footnote in Microsoft Word, you should find the word "Insert a Footnote" in the "Reference" options.

Mistake #6. Tables and figures.

Tables and figures are used in order to visually illustrate data for better comprehension. Students usually make mistakes in formatting table and figure titles and while mentioning the source from where they were taken.

Incorrect Example of a Table Title
Table 1. Correlation between music and language
Source: Molley, Peter. 2014. "Music and Language as Interconnected Notions." *Alabama Journal of Linguistic Sciences* 5 (10): 10-38.
(A table taken from a source)

Here, the author provides the information on the source right after the table title. In Chicago NB style you should mention the table title (after the word "Table 1."), insert the table, and mention the source below. The word "Source" has to be italicized ("Chicago/Turabian: Tables and Figures").

Correct Example of a Table Title
Table 1. Correlation between music and language *(A table taken from a source)* *Source:* Molley, Peter. 2014. "Music and Language as Interconnected Notions." *Alabama Journal of Linguistic Sciences* 5 (10): 10-38.

Figures have to be cited as well, although in a different manner. See the examples below.

Incorrect
Figure 1. Interrelation between society and personal perception of happiness *(A figure taken from a source)* *Source:* White, Andrew. 2017. *Happiness.* 1st ed., 24. New York, US: Balington.

Remember that the information on the figure title and the source have to be shown after the figure itself.

Correct
(A figure taken from a source) Figure 1. Interrelation between society and personal perception of happiness *Source:* White, Andrew. 2017. *Happiness.* 1st ed., 24. New York, US: Balington.

Chicago NB Style is the most minimalistic in relation to others, as it mostly calls to pay significant attention to the bibliography part rather than to follow other numerous requirements. Concentrate your attention on the most common mistakes demonstrated in this guide to make the formatting process easy. Good luck!

Works Cited

"Chicago/Turabian: Tables and Figures." *Boundless*, 2017.

      https://www.boundless.com/writing/textbooks/boundless-writing-textbook/writing-a-paper-

      in-chicago-turabian-style-history-257/chicago-turabian-structure-and-formatting-of-specific-

      elements-324/chicago-turabian-tables-and-figures-354-16934/.

Clements, Jessica, et al. "Chicago Manual of Style 16th Edition." *The Purdue Owl*. Purdue U

      Writing Lab, 07 Feb. 2015. https://owl.english.purdue.edu/owl/resource/717/01/.

"Library Guides: Citing and Referencing: Chicago." *Guides.Lib.Monash.edu*, 2017,

      http://guides.lib.monash.edu/citing-referencing/chicago.

2.4. Mistakes to Avoid in Turabian Format

Turabian Style is commonly used to write essays on history, the arts, and literature ("Turabian Citation Guide"). The formatting is similar to Chicago, which is usually quite confusing for students. Nevertheless, the two styles have significant differences, which are described in the following guide. Please pay attention to the most common mistakes made while formatting with Turabian Style to avoid them in your assignments.

Mistake #1. General guidelines.

You should keep in mind that general guidelines require you to be precise with the details and pay attention to margins, font, and spacing. Please, follow the criteria listed below to fit basic formatting requirements:

- Times New Roman font, 12 pt.

- Black font.

- 1-inch margins on all sides.

- Double-spaced text.

Please take into account that each style (Chicago, Turabian, Harvard, APA, MLA) has similar general guidelines as listed above. Follow the chapter on APA style to avoid general guideline mistakes.

Mistake #2. Running head.

The following point is essential while writing an essay in Turabian style. The mistake deals with inserting a running head at the top of the sheet, even though the style has nothing to do with a running head. Please look at the example below and remember that while formatting your paper according to Turabian Style, you need to mention the page number only.

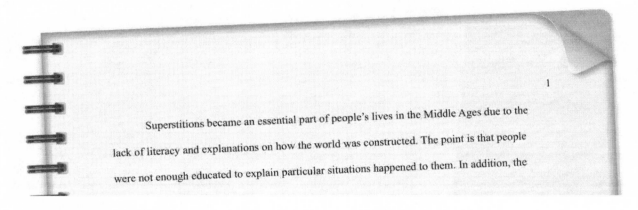

Mistake #3. Title page.

Due to the fact that there are diverse formatting styles, students often make mistakes while creating the title page. The Turabian style requires bold letters in the title instead of italicized. All the rest information should be mentioned due to the scheme:

- First name, last name.
- Class.
- Date (month, date, year).

Check out the next example:

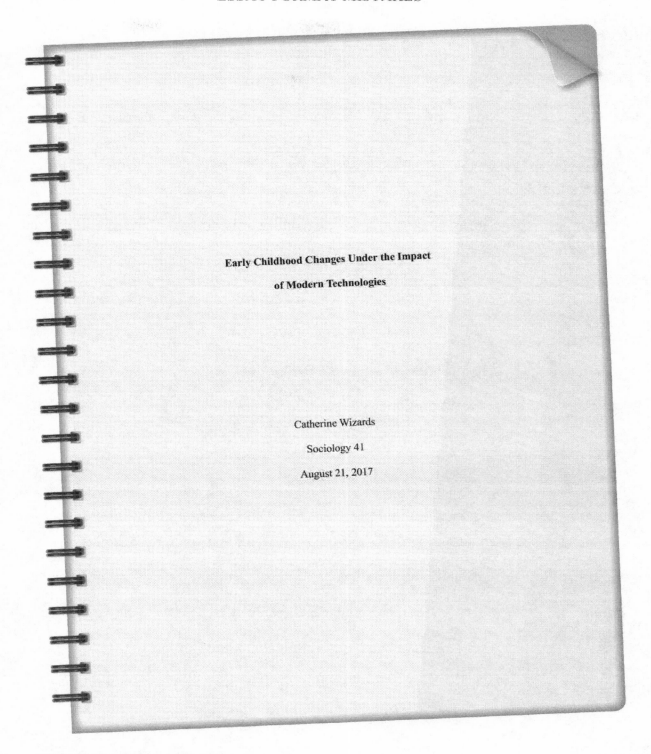

Early Childhood Changes Under the Impact

of Modern Technologies

Catherine Wizards

Sociology 41

August 21, 2017

Mistake #4. Bibliography.

A bibliography in Turabian is similar to Chicago NB style. You should start your reference

list with the word "Bibliography" (not italicised, highlighted, or bold). Then, use the table provided

below to ensure your used sources are correctly formatted.

Journal Articles

Reference Type	Referenced Source
Electronic journal article (including DOI)	Strinic, Visnja. "Arguments in Support and against Euthanasia." *British Journal of Medicine and Medical Research* 9, no. 7 (2015): 1-12.
Printed article	Samah, Irza Hanie Abu, Intan Maizura Abd Rashid, Mohd Juraij Abd Rani, Nor Irwani Abdul Rahman, Muhammad Ahmar Ali, and Muhammad Fazlee Sham Abdullah. "The Roles of Price Perception and Physical Environment in Determining Customer Loyalty: Evidence from Fast Food Restaurant of Malaysia." *International Journal of Development Research* 5, no. 5 (2015): 4366-4370.

Books

Reference Type	Referenced Source
1 author	Chittister, Joan. *Happiness*. 1st ed. Grand Rapids: Wm. B. Eerdmans Publishing Co, 2013.
2 authors	Weber, Max, and Anketell Matthew Henderson. *Max Weber*. 2nd ed. Mansfield Centre, CT: Martino Publishing, 2012.
3-7 authors	Oxlade, Chris, Andrew Farrow, Adam Miller, and Vaarunika Dharmapala. *Modern Medicine*. 1st ed. Chicago, Ill.: Raintree, 2013.
8 or more authors	Bourn, Douglas, Vanessa Andreotti, Barbara Asbrand, David Hicks, Anna Luise Laycock, Alison Leonard, Annette Scheunpflug, and Gillian Temple. *Development Education*. London: Institute of Education Press, 2012.
Chapter of an	Hatten, Timothy S. "Small Business Finance." In *Small Business*

edited book	*Management: Entrepreneurship and beyond*, 220-245. 6th ed. Boston, USA: Cengage Learning, 2016.

Online Sources

Reference Type	Referenced Source
Webpage	Ramos, Annie. "Chile's President Responds to Girl's Dramatic Plea – CNN." *CNN*. Last modified 2015. Accessed August 25, 2017. http://edition.cnn.com/2015/03/01/americas/chile-girl-euthanasia-request/.
Video	*The Psychology of Self-Motivation	Scott Geller	Tedxvirginiatech*. Video. https://www.youtube.com/watch?V=7Sxpkhibr0e, 2013.
Blog	*Nieh, Kylan. "Starting Your First Job Search on Linkedin." Blog, 2017. Accessed August 25, 2017. Https://Blog.Linkedin.Com/2017/August/17/Starting-Your-First-Job-Search.*

* You may compare the sources referenced above with the ones mentioned in the chapters on APA, MLA, and Chicago Styles.

Mistake #5. Footnotes.

The primary feature of Turabian style concerns the utilization of footnotes, or endnotes. This is the main difference between Chicago and Turabian styles, as in Chicago style, you should start a footnote with an appropriate number, while in Turabian you start with a superscript number (Clements, et al. "Chicago Manual of Style 16th Edition"). Have a look at the example below.

Chicago style footnote:

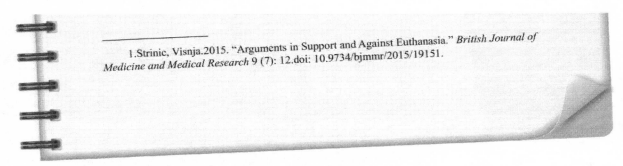

Turabian style footnote:

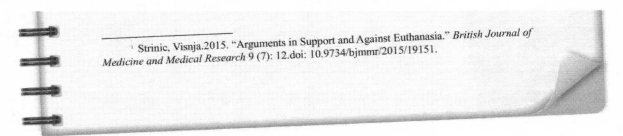

Usually, students make the same mistake while citing a source in footnotes and endnotes. The point is that they copy the resource from the bibliography list and put it into the footnote repeating it each time it appears in the text. Nevertheless, Turabian style requires shortening of the resource titles in case they are used more than once in the essay. Look at the example illustrated below.

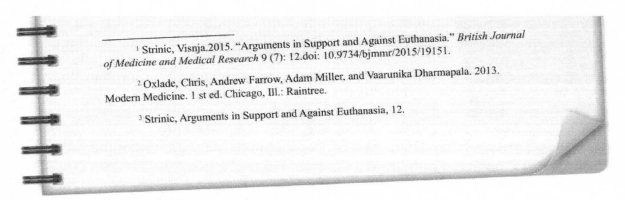

Here, the third reference is shortened to the last name of the author, article title, and page. If you use a source more than twice, you should mention the word "Ibid.," and a page number after it as in the next example (Clements et al. "Chicago Manual of Style 16th Edition").

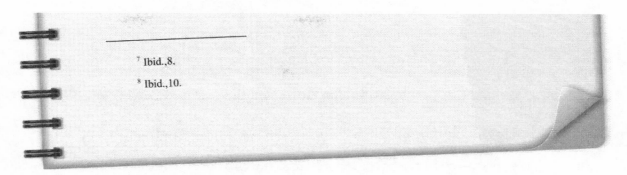

The issues you need to keep in mind while formatting footnotes are as follows ("Library Guides: Citing and Referencing: Chicago"):

- Intended first line of a footnote.

- An extra line space between the footnotes.

- Use "Ibid., (page number)" in case you use the same source often throughout your essay.

Tip: In case you are confused with how to insert a footnote in Microsoft Word, you should find the word "Insert a Footnote" in the "Reference" options.

Mistake #6. Tables and figures.

Tables and figures have to be properly cited as well as any other data piece retrieved from the academic source. The style of citing tables and figures in Turabian is the same as in Chicago NB. You may follow the guidelines in the previous chapter on Chicago style.

Turabian seems to be similar to Chicago style, but it has its own peculiarities. Our guide presents all of them in order to make the writing process easier and the outcomes more satisfactory. Good luck!

Works Cited

Clements, Jessica, et al. "Purdue OWL: Chicago Manual of Style 16th Edition." *The Purdue Owl*.

    Purdue U Writing Lab, 7 Feb. 2014. https://owl.english.purdue.edu/owl/resource/717/01/.

"Library Guides: Citing and Referencing: Chicago." *Guides.Lib.Monash.edu*, 2017,

    http://guides.lib.monash.edu/citing-referencing/chicago.

"Turabian Citation Guide." *Press.Uchicago.edu*, 2017,

    http://www.press.uchicago.edu/books/turabian/turabian_citationguide.html.

Chapter 3. Main Grammatical Mistakes in Essay Writing

Proper grammar is an essential element while grading an essay. This part of writing seems to be the most troublesome for students. They usually do not spend much time drilling this subject and tend to get lower grades because of poor grammar. Nevertheless, by learning common grammatical mistakes, you will be able to achieve high-quality writing and increase the chances to get an "A" for the writing part of any course. The following section will explain four typical types of grammatical mistakes and how to avoid them.

Mistake #1. Spelling mistakes.

1. Complement/Compliment.

Incorrect:

After visiting the beauty salon, Vicky's boyfriend was very generous with complements.	*She has complimented her writing with some illustrations.*

The mentioned words are easy to confuse as they have the same pronunciation. If you make compliments, you admire the appearance of someone or express your appraisal for doing something good ("Compliment or Complement?"). If two things complement each other, it means that they function better together and contribute something necessary to each other so that the overall process could be understood more easily.

Correct:

After visiting the beauty salon, Vicky's boyfriend was very generous with compliments.	*She has complemented her book with some illustrations.*

2. Loose/Lose.

Incorrect:

I could loose Steward's keys tonight if I set them down carelessly.	*Try not to loose my book in a journey.*

According to the dictionary, "loose" serves as an adjective with the meaning "not too tight," which allows you to move freely. "Lose" means to be without something that was formerly in possession. The easiest way to remember the difference between these two words is to remember that one with the meaning "not too tight" has a double "o."

Correct:

I could lose Steward's keys tonight if I set them down carelessly.	Try not to lose my book on a journey.

3. Accept/Except.

Incorrect:

Before excepting his invitation, she needed to check her schedule for the next week.	*Each employee got the Christmas gift accept me.*

"Accept" and "except" are the most confused words among students. "Accept" acts as a verb with the meaning "to receive or admit." "Except" can be seen as a verb and mean "to exclude or leave out," as a preposition (mean "excluding"), and as a conjunction (meaning "other than"). It might be difficult to determine which one to use as they are pronounced the same way. Therefore, you should identify the part of speech you need and then write the appropriate word.

Correct:

Before accepting his invitation, she needed to check her schedule for the next week.	*Each employee got the present except me.*

4. Advice/Advise.

Incorrect:

Jennifer preferred not to take into consideration Lion's advise and acted on her own.	*I usually accept Julia's advises as she is more experienced in such deals.*

"Advice" (noun) is a general recommendation or suggestion given from one person to another, while "advise" (verb) is to give council when the other person is about to make a decision ("Advice vs Advise"). This pair of words is quite easy to recognize as it is very simple to remember that "advice" with a "c" is a noun, while "advise" with an "s" is a verb. Bear in mind that advice is an uncountable noun, thus can be used only in the singular form.

Correct:

Jennifer preferred not to take into consideration Lion's advice and acted on her own.	*I usually accept Julia's advice as she is more experienced in such deals.*

5. Principal/Principle.

Incorrect:

The principle strategy in business is to maintain corporate social responsibility.	*The fundamental principals that we learn at school is honesty and dignity.*

When using the word "principle" (noun), you should remember that it means "general idea or truth" which is based on some argumentation ("Principle vs. Principal"). In contrary, "principal" as an adjective means "the most important." The word "principal" is also a person who heads a school or some organization.

Correct:

The principal strategy in business is to maintain corporate social responsibility.	*The fundamental principles that we learn at school are honesty and dignity.*

Mistake #2. Punctuation mistakes.

This section of the guide will reveal some common mistakes in punctuation in English. Students as well as native speakers sometimes forget some general rules of commas, colons, and semicolons in the sentence. There are several essential recommendations for students to avoid punctuation mistakes with examples included.

1. Transitional words and phrases followed by comma.

Incorrect:

Moreover training is an essential part of increasing the productivity at the workplace.	*To be a good interpreter students should have regular communication with native speakers.*

When you start your sentence with an introductory word or phrase, you should separate it with a comma. "Besides," "moreover," "thus," "therefore," "however," "on the one hand," "on the other hand," and other transitional words are necessary to be separated. In the second example, there is an introductory phrase which should be followed by a comma as well.

Correct:

Moreover, training is an essential part of increasing the productivity at the workplace.	*To be a good interpreter, students should have regular communication with native speakers.*

2. Additional information in the sentence.

Incorrect:

Students who participated in the annual survey of the college were allowed to pass exams two weeks earlier.	*After analyzing the offer which was probably the most crucial in his life John has decided to reject it due to various reasons.*

As you can see from the examples, unnecessary information in the sentence should be separated with commas. These clauses usually exist as independent units and can be omitted without changing the overall sense of the sentence.

Correct:

Students, who participated in the annual survey of the college, were allowed to pass exams two weeks earlier.	*After analyzing the offer, which was probably the most crucial in his life, John has decided to reject it due to various reasons.*

3. Comma in noun clause in narration.

Incorrect:

Jack's mother found, that his bad marks at school were caused by his recent mental disorder.	*After the accident at school, he did not mention, that he had reasons for the lateness.*

It is a common mistake for students to separate noun clauses in the sentence. It is important to mention that if you have doubts about comma separation, you can check the sentence by putting "the idea" before "that." For instance, "A teacher was distraught when he heard the idea that students missed the event." When this phrase makes sense within the sentence, then there is no need to separate it with commas.

Correct:

Jack's mother found that his bad marks at school were caused by his recent mental disorder.	*After the accident at school, he did not mention that he had reasons for the lateness.*

4. Colons at the end of a main clause.

Incorrect:

Before graduating from high school, he had three options to choose from, go to college or start up a business.	*I have decided not to move to New York as I planned, I got a job offer in Boston.*	*Back in 2012, Ruth was not sure about her divorce, she could not believe that they came up to this decision.*

A colon is used when the sentence seems to be completed, but you have decided to add some information to it ("Colons, Semicolons and Dashes"). There are three occasions when a colon is appropriate in the sentence: when there is a list, elaboration, or restatement.

Correct:

Before graduating from high school, he had three options to choose from: go to college or start up a business.	*Recently, I have decided not to move to New York as I planned: I got a job offer in Boston.*	*Back in 2012, Ruth was not sure about her divorce: she could not believe that they came up to this decision.*

5. Semicolon usage.

Incorrect:

I am going to purchase this item, however, I will ask Clarissa for advice.	*When I have attended the conference, I have met some influential people, such as Mr. Robinson, the HR chief, Mrs Rebecca, supply chain manager, and Ms. Valencia, manager of the R&D department.*	*Cooking courses gave the opportunity for Jack and Samantha to learn new recipes of Italian cuisine, they mastered techniques of cooking as such.*

The semicolon is often confused with a comma. It is used when we need to separate two independent parts of the sentence ("Colons, Semicolons and Dashes"). In most cases, these elements are related to each other, but the second one does not serve as a clarification of the first. In the table below, there are three occasions when you can use a semicolon as punctuation. In the first example, we use a semicolon as the second independent clause starts with "however" (which is a conjunctive adverb). It might also start with "moreover," "therefore," "otherwise," "consequently," and other adverbs. In the second example, we use a semicolon when we need to separate two items in the list with a comma. Therefore, list components are better visible when you separate them with a semicolon. The last example shows that by using a semicolon, we can join two independent clauses in one sentence.

Correct:

I am going to purchase this item; however, I will ask Clarissa for advice.	When I have attended the conference, I have met some influential people, such as Mr. Robinson, the HR chief; Mrs. Rebecca, supply chain manager; and Ms. Valencia, manager of the R&D department.	Cooking courses gave the opportunity for Jack and Samantha to learn new recipes of Italian, French, and German cuisine; they mastered techniques of preparing as such.

6. Apostrophe usage.

Incorrect:

Janet friend has been trying to reach her last night.	One of the fundamental aspects of this experiment is not to ignore it's principal rules.

The apostrophe in English is used only in two cases: when we want to present possession and for a contraction. The latter is prohibited in writing formal and academic papers; however, it is important not to confuse these types ("How to Use Apostrophes"). If the noun is used in the singular form and you need to show possession, we use "'s." When the word is in plural form and ends in "s," we just put an apostrophe at the end of the word. Contraction forms are used with an apostrophe and are easy to remember so not to confuse. These are "it's" (it is, or it has), "don't" (do not), "doesn't" (does not), "they're" (they are), and others.

Correct:

Janet's friend has been trying to reach her last night.	*One of the fundamental aspects of this experiment is not to ignore its principal rules.*

7. Dashes.

Incorrect:

James wanted all of us, Joann, Clark, and William, to go to Camel Beach.	*We traveled around France, and met Tina, whom I have not seen for seven years.*

A dash is mainly used to make an emphasis on the additional information. Then, you can also use dashes when you want to surprise the reader with some information. However, using dashes in formal writing is considered to be inappropriate ("Colons, Semicolons and Dashes"). You can also use a dash when you summarize the idea of the sentence. For instance: "History, mathematics, chemistry, and English—these are some basic disciplines each student can choose from."

Correct:

James wanted all of us—Joann, Clark, and William—to go to Camel Beach.	*We traveled around France—and met Tina, whom I have not seen for seven years.*

Mistake #3. Word order.

Word order plays an essential role in English. The relations of words in the sentence is shown by their position, not their form. Therefore, word order in English remains inflexible and fixed. You cannot change the places of certain words in a sentence, the subject and object in particular.

1. Standard word order.

Incorrect:

Recently, Janis and her husband an apartment bought.	*An English course took she at her new school.*

The most uncomplicated word order is Subject+Verb+Object, or SVO. It is easy for you to remember by breaking the sentence into sections and determining the correct order. This type of mistake is the rarest but sometimes occurs among students (M. Paiz, Joshua et al.). If you need to make a negative sentence, the same word order is maintained, where it goes before the main verb and after the auxiliary verb. (For instance: "They did not follow all the instructions in the manual.")

Correct:

Recently, Janis and her husband bought an apartment.	*She took an English course at her new school.*

2. Word order in questions.

Incorrect:

I should accept his offer concerning guiding the case he currently works on?	*You did find the conference concerning new educational methods useful?*

There are two standard methods for asking a question; these are auxiliary verb and modal verb+subject+verb. It is important to remember for the student that the modal verb can change the form while the auxiliary never changes the form.

Correct:

Should I accept his offer concerning guiding the case he currently works on?	*Did you find the conference concerning new educational methods useful?*

3. Inverted word order.

Incorrect:

> *You have not any "A" marks for this course?*

Inversion in English is constructed by placing the subject after the predicate. There are some occasions when you can apply an inversion. Firstly, when you want to make an emphasis by using the adverb at the beginning of the sentence, as the order of words often used in formal writing. (Never have I ever wanted to become a vegetarian.) Secondly, you can also use the inversion after "here-there" and "not" at the beginning of the sentence. (Not till I saw her did I believe that she had changed her haircut. When I came to the hospital, there was John, waiting for me with flowers.)

Correct:

> *Haven't you got any "A" marks for this course?*

4. Misplacing the modifiers.

Incorrect:

Michael and Alice, who was late to the interview, were waiting for the candidate.	*The members of the crew were expecting the passengers, who were completely exhausted from the previous flight.*

The problem of misplaced modifiers is that students position modifiers too far from the word that should be described (Simmons, Robin). This mistake can ruin the overall sense of the sentence, thus the interpretation is misunderstood. In order to solve such a mistake, you should consider which part of the sentence you are describing and place the modifier closer to it.

Correct:

Michael and Alice were waiting for the candidate, who was late to the interview.	*The members of the crew, who were completely exhausted from the previous flight, were expecting the passengers.*

Mistake #4. Subject-verb agreement.

The last part of the guide is dedicated to the most troublesome part of English. Subject-verb agreement is considered to be the most difficult for students.

1. Verb agreement with the subject number and person.

Incorrect:

Alex have been doing excellent work with the business, until the crisis in 2007.	*They cleans the house twice a month.*

The basic rule of subject-verb agreement is that a singular subject requires a singular form of the verb. If the subject is third form singular, you will need to find agreement with the proper verb, which, in the present tense, ends on "-s" (-es). First and second person do not require the ending of the verb.

Correct:

Alex has been doing excellent work with the business, until the crisis in 2007.	*They clean the house twice a month.*

2. Indefinite subject.

Incorrect:

Everyone were excited to visit the exhibition of modern paintings in this small town.	*Nobody were happy about the news concerning policies within the corporation.*

It is a common mistake among students to confuse indefinite subjects and treat those as a plural form. You should remember that "anybody," "anyone," "everyone," "nobody," "someone," "each," "anything," and "everything" are the singular form of the subject.

Note! **"All," "any," "none,"** and **"some"** can be in both singular and plural form, which depends on the noun or pronoun that they refer to. For instance: "None of the recommendations were considered by the employees."

Correct:

Everyone was excited to visit the exhibition of modern paintings in this small town.	*Nobody was happy about the news concerning policies within the corporation.*

3. Two subjects connected with "and."

Incorrect:

He and his friends was at the welcome party last night.	*Neither the dress nor the skirt were accepted by Jennifer.*

When in the sentence you connect two subjects using "and," the verb must be in the plural form. However, when two singular nouns (subjects) are connected with "or" (nor), the singular form of a verb is required.

Note! When you connect subjects which are both singular and plural, the verb with the nearest subject to the verb should be in agreement. For example: "His friend and some colleagues were glad to meet him after the hospital. Some of his colleagues and his friend was glad to meet him after the hospital."

Correct:

He and his friends were at the welcome party last night.	*Neither the dress nor the skirt was accepted by Jennifer.*

4. An agreement with the subject, and not the phrase between S-V.

Incorrect:

The executive of the company, as well as all the employees, follow the regulations of the firm.	*John, with all his dogs, were having a long walk in the park.*

Do not become confused when you have the phrase between the subject and the verb (M. Paiz, Joshua et al.). You should identify the subject and have it agree with the verb, not the expression between.

Correct:

The executive of the company, as well as all the employees, follows the regulations of the firm.	*John, with all his dogs, was having a long walk in the park while his wife was visiting a doctor.*

5. Collective nouns.

Incorrect:

The family were happy to be on the holiday together.	*The crew were preparing to meet all the passengers in business class appropriately.*

Students become confused while using a collective noun and agree such with the verb as a plural form. However, despite the fact that they include several members, they must be agreed as a singular form of the subject. Some of the collective nouns are "committee," "team," "family," "group," and others.

Correct:

The family was happy to be on holiday together.	*The crew was preparing to meet all the passengers in business class appropriately.*

We have identified some of the most common grammatical mistakes which students make. Analyze the guide carefully in order to avoid such mistakes in your writings. We hope the examples and recommendations will be useful for you. Good luck!

Works Cited

"Advice vs Advise." *E Learn English Language*, 2017.

http://www.elearnenglishlanguage.com/blog/english-mistakes/advice-vs-advise/.

"Colons, Semicolons and Dashes." *Yourdictionary*, 2017.

http://grammar.yourdictionary.com/punctuation/colons-semicolons-and-dashes.html.

"Compliment or Complement?" *Oxfordwords Blog*, 2017.

http://blog.oxforddictionaries.com/2011/04/compliment-or-complement/.

"How to Use Apostrophes." *Scribendi.com*, 2017.

https://www.scribendi.com/advice/using_apostrophes.en.html.

Maddox, Maeve. "Top 10 Punctuation Mistakes." *Daily Writing Tips*, 2017.

https://www.dailywritingtips.com/top-10-punctuation-mistakes/.

M. Paiz, Joshua et al. "Purdue OWL: Subject/Verb Agreement." *The Purdue OWL*. Purdue U

Writing Lab, 1 Apr. 2014. https://owl.english.purdue.edu/owl/resource/599/01/.

"Principle vs Principal." *Oxfordwords Blog*, 2017.

http://blog.oxforddictionaries.com/2011/08/principle-or-principal/.

Simmons, Robin. "Grammar Bytes! The Misplaced Modifier." *Chompchomp.com*, 2017.

http://www.chompchomp.com/terms/misplacedmodifier.htm.

Chapter 4. Stylistic Mistakes in Academic Writing

Most students equate perfect contents, essay structure, and following the format style as the keys to getting the highest grades for written work. Nevertheless, stylistic mistakes do matter and require attention to detail to ensure even the smallest part of the essay fits its overall picture. Stylistic elements are about complementing your essay with sophisticated academic qualities.

In this chapter, we are going to enlighten the most common mistakes related to word choice, commonly confused words, style, and sentence structure. The first part of the guide includes information on how to choose the most suitable words to fulfill the ideas you want to express. Next, we have illustrated the most commonly confused words which may lead to misunderstandings of content. Here, we define the words which you may muddle and, with the help of examples, show a primary difference between such word pairs. Style is a vital element in academic writings, as it impacts the general impression left after reading. You may prove that you can organize arguments and thoughts in a sophisticated way, or you may fail, using improper writing mannerisms and expressions. To conclude the guide, we present you the mistakes students make while structuring sentences, and which may impact their final grades.

Along with mistake descriptions, we have added recommendations on how to avoid them while writing your further essays. Consequently, after reading our guide and taking into consideration all the points discussed, you can be confident that your assignments will be filled with interesting ideas which are described with accurately picked words, structurally correct sentences, and appropriate style. We will show you that stylistic complications may be eliminated in several steps, making the writing process more pleasant and effortless.

4.1. Word Choice Mistakes

While writing an essay, you may face many challenges and choices you have to make. A topic, even with correctly arranged and composed ideas enhanced with a catchy thesis, is not enough to persuade your audience. Word choice is an essential element in essay writing, as it illustrates your ability to use sophisticated language and enhances your arguments. In the following guide, we are going to discuss common word choice mistakes students make and show how to avoid them.

Mistake #1. Weak words.

Weak words are the primary problem of many students as they may provoke the impression of knowledge insufficiency. Also, ideas you want to express may seem unclear for the audience. Please, refer to the example mentioned below.

Example #1. Incorrect: *Samsung has produced many good products.*

The word "good" is weak since it does not specify what exactly it means to be a good product. It may be useful, efficient, long-lasting, or any other variation. In order to make the sentence more concrete, choose the words which would interpret your ideas in a more valuable and specific manner for the reader to make the right conclusions.

Correct: *Samsung has produced a variety of reliable and long-lasting products.*

Example #2. Incorrect: *If you want to eat tasty food, go to McDonald's.*

In the shown example, the word "tasty" is too general. The point is that you need to impact the readers and convince them with properly chosen words. Instead of "tasty" in the particular example, you may use other words as in the corrected version below.

Correct: *If you want to eat delicious food following a unique recipe, go to McDonald's.*

Mistake #2. Overly complex terms.

This kind of mistake is commonly made by students as they think that complicated terms in the essay make it look advanced ("Word Choice"). Nevertheless, this method often makes an essay challenging to perceive, leaving the reader with no conclusions made. For example:

Incorrect: *The author utilized feminist perspectives through the prism of dialectal interface among the initial protagonistic group.*

The mentioned example illustrates the mix of diverse terms which, as a result, may not send a concrete and clear message to the reader. Students often want to sound smart, but there is no sense behind peppering each sentence with complex words. In order to avoid sentence overload, use plain words in combination with terms necessary to cover the topic.

Correct: *Protagonists with diverse dialectal peculiarities illustrated the author's feministic disposition.*

Tip: In case you are not sure that your essay is understandable enough, refer to other students or your relatives. They may read your paper and tell you whether they perceived the information. This will help you find out the weaknesses of your essay.

Mistake #3. Repetition.

Students often choose correct words which fit the context, although they put them twice or three times into one sentence. Moreover, the same words may be noticed ten or more times throughout the essay. Repetition of words indicates the lack of a broad vocabulary which may decrease the final essay grade. Look at the example below.

Incorrect: *An educational institution is a place where people get an education in order to enter educated parts of the society.*

You may notice that the word "education" and its derivations are used too often in one sentence. If you have difficulties with vocabulary and cannot think of the most relevant synonym, you may use dictionaries to find the most appropriate variants and avoid this kind of mistake.

Correct: *An educational institution is a place where people receive knowledge in order to become valuable parts of an erudite society.*

Mistake #4. Misused words.

Sometimes, students try to make the essay look more sophisticated with the usage of "smart" words without trying to find out even the meaning of those words ("Word Choice"). The context and final impression of the essay may be ruined if a student inserted words with which he or she is not familiar. Refer to the example demonstrated below.

Incorrect: *He found it ironic to lose a passport the day before the trip.*

In this particular example, the word "ironic" is used incorrectly, as there is a difference between the words "ironic" and "coincidental," and the writer intended for the latter understanding. This improper usage would cause the reader to misunderstand the meaning of the sentence and doubt whether the writer is intelligent enough to know the meaning of the used words, and in some cases, whether there was some other meaning that they did not quite understand through the context. You may say something is ironic when the result is amusing and unusual, yet more than coincidental. "Coincidental" is used to describe a situation which is unpredictable and which happened by chance.

Correct: *He found it coincidental to lose a passport the day before the trip.*

The lexical content of an essay is vital since it completes the final impression after reading. In addition, whether too complicated or straightforward, words may be confusing for the audience, provoking incorrect conclusions. Repeated words and words which are utilized without having an idea of their meaning are bad habits to avoid as well. Please, take into consideration the main mistakes in word choice to eliminate them in your essays. Good luck!

Works Cited

"Why Good Writing Is All about Good Word Choice." *Thoughtco*, 2017.

https://www.thoughtco.com/word-choice-composition-1692500.

"Word Choice." *The Writing Center*, 2017. http://writingcenter.unc.edu/tips-and-tools/word-choice/.

4.2. Commonly Confused Words

The English language has a variety of word meanings, and even more synonyms to them. Due to the fact that the linguistic system is broad, there are certain word groups which include, as you may think, the same base words or sounds. Nevertheless, while writing academic papers, students often get lower grades for the lexical content of their essays as a result of the incorrect words used. The following part of the guide is about to explain the difference between the most confusing words in English in order to ease your writing process.

Mistake #1. Homonyms.

Homonyms are words which may be confusing for both native speakers and international students. The idea is that homonyms are the words which sound and are spelled similarly, but have polar meanings. We have created a list of the most commonly used homonyms to explain their difference and illustrate examples of their correct utilization.

1. Address.

Railroad 14 is an address where Richard Routh used to live.	*Richard Routh addressed his wife with unique tenderness.*

The idea of the mentioned examples is the opposing meanings of the words regarding sentence context. Note that the first example shows the word "address" (noun) as a location. "Address" (verb) in the second sentence means "to speak to" ("Examples of Homonyms").

2. Current.

The current state of the Indian market remains steady.	*Margaret was standing at the seashore when a current of ocean water swept her off her feet.*

Try not to confuse the meaning of the words mentioned above. In the first example, "current" (adjective) means up to date or present time, and in the second, "current" (noun) means a flow of water ("Examples of Homonyms").

3. Pound.

The woman set a record as her weight was about 200 pounds.	*George pounded him to show that no one could offend his wife.*

In order not to make yourself confused with the words used above, remember that they are different in meaning. "Pound" (noun) in the first example is a unit of weight, and in the second, "pound" (verb) equals "to beat" ("Examples of Homonyms").

4. Match.

She chose black shoes to match her blouse.	*In case you are going to camp, it is better to take a lighter instead of matches.*

The first example illustrates that the word "match" in the particular context means "to pair like items." In the second one, "matches" means "wooden sticks to make a flame" ("Examples of Homonyms").

Mistake #2. Homophones.

Homophones are words which sound the same, although have diverse meanings and spelling. Please refer to the examples illustrated below to understand the difference between homophones and use them correctly in your essays.

1. Accept/Except.

Incorrect:

Each scientist considered the theory as a failure accept him.	*Annet Winfred was excepted to the national university in 1945.*

The main mistake here concerns a misuse of the words, as "accept" is a verb (to agree) and "except" (not including) is a conjunction ("Word Choice In Academic Writing: Commonly Confused English Words").

Correct:

Each scientist considered the theory as a failure except him.	*Annet Winfred was accepted to the national university in 1945.*

2. Affect/Effect.

Incorrect:

The disaster had a tremendous affect on the life of thousands.	*The disaster tremendously effected the life of thousands.*

Remember that the word "affect" is a verb (to influence, to impact) and "effect" is a noun (the result) ("Word Choice in Academic Writing: Commonly Confused English Words").

Correct:

The disaster had a tremendous effect on the life of thousands.	*The disaster tremendously affected the life of thousands.*

3. Practice/Practise.

Incorrect:

Students should practice their writing skills.	*Practise means doing something on a regular basis.*

The mistake deals with the wrong utilization of the words as parts of speech. "Practice" is a noun (preparation) and "practise" is a verb (to prepare). Please note that this example applies primarily to British English, and not American English.

Correct:

Students should practise their writing skills.	*Practice is a noun which means doing something on a regular basis.*

4. Then/Than.

Incorrect:

The man preferred using the qualitative method rather then quantitative.	*Than, the scientist announced the hypothesis he had been working on.*

Note that "then" is an adverb, meaning "at a previous time," as well as also meaning "next," and "than" is a conjunction which is used mainly for comparisons ("Word Choice in Academic Writing: Commonly Confused English Words").

Correct:

The man preferred using the qualitative method rather than the quantitative.	*Then, the scientist announced the hypothesis he had been working on for years.*

Mistake #3. Other commonly confused words.

1. Among/Between.

Incorrect:

The lawyers had found the signed document, between other missing papers.	*The box became the reason for the fight among two community members.*

The mistakes shown above deal with the wrong usage of the words in relation to the sentence context. The conjunction "between" is defined as "internal to, involving specific members." "Among" is a conjunction which is equal to "in the middle of" ("Between Or Among?").

Correct:

The lawyers had found the signed document, among other missing papers.	*The box became the reason for the fight between two community members.*

2. E.g./I.e.

Incorrect:

Scientists often use the quantitative research method (i.e. surveys) to increase data reliability.	*Nowadays, women follow feministic views, e.g. trying to fight for equal rights between males and females.*

The difference between "i.e." and "e.g." is usually quite confusing for students. However, you should remember that "i.e." means "that is" and "e.g." is "for example" ("Top 30 Commonly Confused Words in English").

Correct:

Scientists often use the quantitative research method (e.g. surveys) to increase data reliability.	*Nowadays, women follow feministic views, i.e. trying to fight for equal rights between males and females.*

3. Historic/Historical.

Incorrect:

Their victory became the new historical event to occur in Chicago.	*Scientists found historic evidence which confirmed an evolution theory.*

The mistake enlightened in the example above considers a misinterpretation of the two, from first sight, similar words. Nevertheless, the context in which the two are used differs. "Historic" stands for something essential and significant. "Historical" means something related to the past or history ("Top 30 Commonly Confused Words in English").

Correct:

Their victory became the new historic event to occur in Chicago.	*Scientists found historical evidence which confirms an evolution theory.*

4. Economic/Economical.

Incorrect:

The economical state of China has been improving in recent years.	*A Ford is considered to be one of the most economic automobiles in the world.*

Here, the meaning of the two words varies significantly. The word "economic" relates to industry and trade. "Economical" is a characteristic of something that does not need much money or resources to be spent on ("Economic Or Economical?").

Correct:

The economic state of China has been improving in recent years.	*A Ford is considered to be one of the most economical automobiles in the world.*

We tried to find the most challenging words which students face while writing essays. Read the guide carefully and notice the difference between confusing words in order to make your text free of such lexical mistakes. Good luck!

Confusing Words to Take Into Account

Accent	Assent
Allude	Elude
Allusion	Illusion
Altar	Alter
Altogether	All together
Among	Amongst
Angel	Angle
Assure	Insure
Beside	Besides
Borrow	Lend
Brake	Break
Capital	Capitol
Cite	Site
Clothes	Cloths
Coarse	Course
Complement	Compliment
Corps	Corpse
Dairy	Diary
Dessert	Desert
Die	Dye
Discrete	Discreet
Elicit	Illicit
Emigrate	Immigrate
Eminent	Imminent

Envelop	Envelope
Fair	Fare
Farther	Further
Forth	Fourth
Heard	Herd
Human	Humane
Lay	Lie
Lead	Led
Lightening	Lightning
Metal	Mettle
Moral	Morale
Peak	Peek
Personal	Personnel
Precede	Proceed
Quiet	Quite
Quote	Quotation
Rain	Rein
Rational	Rationale
Respectfully	Respectively
Stationary	Stationery
Taught	Taut
Through	Thorough
Toward	Towards
Waive	Wave
Weather	Whether

Works Cited

"Between or Among?" *Dictionary.Cambridge.org*, 2017.

http://dictionary.cambridge.org/grammar/british-grammar/between-or-among.

"Economic or Economical?" *Dictionary.Cambridge.org*, 2017.

http://dictionary.cambridge.org/grammar/british-grammar/economic-or-economical.

"Examples of Homonyms." *YourDictionary*, 2017. http://examples.yourdictionary.com/examples-

of-homonyms.html.

"Top 30 Commonly Confused Words in English." *Grammarly Blog*, 2017.

https://www.grammarly.com/blog/commonly-confused-words/.

"Word Choice in Academic Writing: Commonly Confused English Words." *Enago Academy*, 2017.

http://www.enago.com/academy/commonly-confused-english-words/.

4.3. Style Mistakes

Academic writing assignments illustrate your ability to choose a proper style to cover the topic and enhance arguments that are unenlightened. A successful essay has to follow not only grammatical rules and vocabulary and format peculiarities, but stylistic ones as well. Please, take into account the most widespread stylistic mistakes demonstrated below to increase the quality of your paper.

Mistake #1. Sentences ending with prepositions.

Many students use a variety of prepositions at the end of sentences ("Common Stylistic Errors"). The idea itself is acceptable, although most of the essays in which nearly each sentence ends with a preposition deserve a grade decrease due to sentence style similarity.

Incorrect: *The topic of gender inequality became the one they disagreed on.*

In the example below, the preposition "on" stands at the end of the sentence. The mistake is not critical as there is no actual grammatical rule which would forbid such a construction. Nevertheless, it is better to avoid such word order to make an essay stylistically acceptable. Instead, you may insert a preposition in the middle of a sentence.

Correct: *They disagreed on the topic of gender inequality.*

Mistake #2. Informality.

Academic writing requires proper stylistic formatting to confirm the status of the writer as intelligent and academic. Formality is an essential point to be followed in here since essays have to include appropriate terms and descriptions ("Appropriate Language: Overview"). Refer to the example mentioned below.

Incorrect: *She saw a cute but lonely puppy and couldn't stand crying.*

The example above includes two mistakes which increase the level of informality. First of all, the word "cute" is a colorful one which is used in conversational language. You may substitute the word with any other more appropriate version using a dictionary. Secondly, academic writing should not include contractions as they are regarded as more informal. To avoid the mistake, you need to reread your essay and separate contractions into two parts.

Correct: *She saw a beautiful but lonely puppy and could not stand crying.*

Mistake #3. Idiomatic expressions.

Academic essays have to sound credible and formal to make the data more reliable and influential. Idioms are constructions which make an essay look more informal ("Appropriate Language: Overview"). While writing, you need to deeply cover the topic and usage of idiomatic expressions will raise more questions than answers.

Incorrect: *He could not meet the project's deadline as he felt a bit under the weather.*

Here, the idiom emphasizes a high level of informality. You may substitute an idiom with appropriate phrases. In case you have problems with identifying the correct match for the idiom, you may consult a dictionary.

Correct: *He could not meet the project's deadline as he was feeling ill.*

Mistake #4. Passive voice overuse.

Passive constructions are considered to be a tool to make the reader focused on the particular doer of an action ("Elements of Writing: How to Avoid Common Mistakes in Style"). Students often use passive voice as it sounds more sophisticated and provides an illusion of intelligence and overall in-depth investigation of a topic. Nevertheless, students usually try too hard to make an essay look "smart" with the passive voice overuse. See the example below.

Incorrect: *All the theories connected with motivation may be regarded as false. People who were born as ordinary individuals with no leadership skills have been impacted with a short-term inspiration along with motivation which are provided by real leaders.*

The mistake in here deals with passive voice usage, with the occurrence happening even multiple times in the same sentence. Indeed, you may utilize it in your essay, although try not to make all the constructions passive as it may seem like you do not know any other grammatical construction. Instead, you may put the subject in the first place and substitute passive with active voice.

Correct: *All the theories connected with motivation may be regarded as false. Real leaders provide short-term inspiration along with motivation for people born as ordinary individuals with no leadership skills.*

Mistake #5. Typos.

Typos are probably the most common mistake among students. Usually, because of a lack of time, sentences are quickly typed, and the final essay is read in a hurry without noticing surface mistakes.

Incorrect: *Academi writing requites proper attention paid to details to ensdure the overall essay accuracy. Please, follw our guide to inprove your writing skills and to endure yourself that any writing task may be interesting and less complivated.*

You may notice many typos made in the example provided. The only advice in here is to proofread the essay two or three times to check it for typos and correct the spelling.

Correct: *Academic writing requires proper attention paid to details to ensure the overall essay accuracy. Please, follow our guide to improve your writing skills and to ensure yourself that any writing task can become interesting and less complicated.*

We have covered common stylistic mistakes in the guide to assist you while writing your essay. Style is a crucial element for grading your work, so use our advice described in the guide to increase your chances for an "A." Good luck!

Works Cited

"Appropriate Language: Overview." *Owl.English.Purdue.edu*, 2017.

    https://owl.english.purdue.edu/owl/owlprint/608/.

"Common Stylistic Errors." *Qcpages.Qc.Cuny.edu*, 2017.

    http://qcpages.qc.cuny.edu/writing/history/editing/errors.html.

"Elements of Writing: How to Avoid Common Mistakes in Style." *Write.com*, 2017.

    http://www.write.com/elements-of-writing-how-to-avoid-common-mistakes-in-style/.

4.4. Sentence Structure Mistakes

Since essays are constructed from sentences, it is vital to make their structure correct. The idea is that such mistakes are the most common among students, as even while using sophisticated language and a plethora of smart words, the essay may fail because of incorrect sentence composition. In the following guide, we present the most widespread structural mistakes for you to avoid to better persuade your readers in each written sentence.

Mistake #1. Sentences too simple and too short.

The primary mistake concerning sentence structure is the size. Many students consider short sentences as the way to make fewer mistakes, although, as a result, the point of the essay is often not reached. In the case of writing academic essays, you should remember that more complex and longer sentences can illustrate your ability to build arguments logically and generally appear more persuasive.

Incorrect: *Marie Curie wanted to investigate the phenomenon of radioactivity. Finally, she did it.*

The second sentence is grammatically correct, although it does not bring any significant message. Instead, it provokes the feeling of simplicity and lack of writing skills. In order to make a sentence look more complex, you may unite two simple and short ones.

Correct: *Marie Curie succeeded in investigating the phenomenon of radioactivity after years of scientific research.*

Tips: In case you are not sure if a sentence is grammatically correct, you may use grammar checkers ("Most Common Mistakes in ESL Essay Writing"). They may point out the weak places of your essay and ensure you should rewrite separate parts of it. However, pay attention, because spelling and grammar checkers cannot guarantee you that all the mistakes are cut off.

As well, students often write uninformative sentences using construction that is too simple. Look at the example mentioned below.

Incorrect: *Police arrested him for a robbery.*

The mentioned example shows that the sentence is too simply constructed. You should remember that more accurate details may help you make the data more convincing and get a higher grade for your paper as a result.

Correct: *The man was accused of a robbery and arrested by the police the following day.*

Mistake #2. Sentence fragments.

In this section, we are going to discuss the second common mistake, which is related to vast utilization of sentence fragments. According to the basic rules of grammar of the English language, each sentence requires a predicate and a subject ("Sentence Fragments"). Nevertheless, sometimes students neglect the rule and write sentence fragments with a lonely standing verb or subject.

Example #1. Incorrect: *Since smoking cigarettes has a variety of detrimental effects on health.*

The mistake demonstrates the incompleteness of the sentence. The fragment is grammatically incorrect and, in addition, does not bring the fully covered point to the reader, lacking sense. In order to avoid the mistake, make sure that all of your sentences have a subject and predicate.

Correct: *Since smoking cigarettes has a variety of detrimental effects on health, it has to be forbidden among members of society.*

Example #2. Incorrect: *The idea which crossed his mind.*

Here, the reader can hardly find out what the idea was and which impact it caused. Such a sentence raises more questions than answers. To avoid the mistake, you need to proofread the essay written and ask yourself whether each sentence has a completed idea which is logically covered, and grammatically and structurally enhanced.

Correct: *The idea which crossed his mind became the newly discovered gravity theory.*

Mistake #3. Run-ons.

Run-ons are two clauses of a sentence which are not correctly connected ("Run-On Sentences, Comma Splices"). This kind of mistake is widespread and causes misunderstandings of the message sent.

Incorrect: *I read the guide on the most common mistakes in academic essays I improved my skills.*

The sentence above demonstrates the improper usage of two independent clauses. In order to make them structurally fit each other, you may choose one of the following ways of their accurate connection.

Correct: Variant #1: *I read the guide on the most common mistakes in academic essays, and I improved my skills.* (inserted comma + conjunction)

Variant #2: *I read the guide on the most common mistakes in academic essays; I improved my skills as a result.* (inserted semi colon + second phrase revision)

Variant #3: *I have read the guide on the most common mistakes in academic essays. As a result, I improved my skills.* (two separate sentences)

The variant you choose depends on the tone you want to express. In the first case, the sentence looks more conversational with no stress on the second part of it. Nevertheless, in the second and third variants, you will put an emphasis on the validity of both sentences. This way, you will sound more confident in the words you write and arguments you support. Note that in the third variant with sentence separation, the short sentence does make sense and is used to put a stress on the particular information. However, try to develop each sentence further to avoid having your essay look too simple.

Mistake #4. Comma splice.

In order to make essays look more complicated and ideas more complexly expressed, students often combine two or even three sentences into one. Indeed, the method may be utilized to sound more persuasive and sophisticated, although they should be combined with the usage of comma and a conjunction as, in another case, it is not grammatically correct ("Run-On Sentences, Comma Splices"). Please, refer to the example mentioned below.

Example #1. Incorrect: *The man pushed her he did not even apologize.*

Here, you may see the example of a comma splice as the two complete sentences are not joined correctly. Consider the first part and the second part separately: "The man pushed her" and "he did not even apologize." Since each of the clauses does not depend on the other, while combining them, you should insert a comma and a conjunction.

Correct: *The man pushed her, but he did not even apologize.*

Example #2. Incorrect: *The man pushed her he did not even apologize.*

The mistake is the same as in the previous example, although there is one more way to fix it. If you are not sure on how to correctly combine the two clauses, you may just put a period and start a new sentence.

Correct: *The man pushed her. He did not even apologize.*

Sentence structure does matter while writing your essay. The point is that even from first glance you may notice whether thoughts and arguments are expressed in an academic way or an amateurish manner. In order to make your paper look more complete and free of sentence structure mistakes, take the information mentioned above into account. Good luck!

Works Cited

"Most Common Mistakes in ESL Essay Writing." *Italki.com*, 2017.

    https://www.italki.com/article/973/Most-Common-Mistakes-In-ESL-Essay-Writing.

"Run-On Sentences, Comma Splices." *Grammar.Ccc.Commnet.edu*, 2017.

    http://grammar.ccc.commnet.edu/grammar/runons.htm.

"Sentence Fragments." *Grammarly Blog*, 2017. https://www.grammarly.com/blog/mistake-of-the-

    month-sentence-fragments/.

"Writing Essays for Dummies." May, 2017. https://essayshark.com/blog/writing-essays-for-

    dummies/

Chapter 5. Mistakes in Following Essay Structure and Requirements

Different types of essays require specific rules to follow concerning their structure. Each of them includes the introduction and the summary part; nevertheless, the body varies according to the requirements of the particular kind of writing. This section of the guide will demonstrate the most common mistakes students make while composing an essay. Here, you will also find some recommendations on how to avoid such mistakes.

5.1. Compare and Contrast Essay

A compare and contrast essay is one of the types of academic writings which may be possessed as an independent type of essay or a part of a larger paper. In general, the comparison part is devoted to finding the similarities between the two issues, while the contrast section identifies the differences between particular things ("Compare & Contrast Essays"). Usually, students are ordered to write such an essay to present the understanding of methods, literature genres, strategies, approaches, etc. Typically, you may choose how to structure your essay: you may list the similarities and differences of two issues one by one or separate the similarities and differences of one notion and then repeat the same for the other.

Mistake #1. Transition elements.

Incorrect: *Knowledge is a small part of wisdom. There is a difference between those terms which may be impressive. When people talk about learning, they mean the process of finding facts and information. Individuals obtain new knowledge every day even while walking down the street or talking to other people. The human brain tends to absorb every piece of information promptly and collect it in memory.*

As you may see from the example, there are no transitional elements which would connect sentences building one general idea of the paragraph. The reader should understand the link among all the sentences to catch the sense of the comparison and contrast. Try to include linking phrases and words when you start a new idea within the paragraph and when you change the topic moving to the next one. Using this method, the reader obtains a clear sequence of your thoughts and understands the compare/contrast part of the essay.

Correct: *Knowledge is a small part of wisdom; however, there is a difference between those terms which may be impressive. Therefore, when people talk about learning, they mean the process of finding facts and information. Individuals obtain new knowledge every day even while walking down the street or talking to other people. As a result, the human brain tends to absorb every piece of information promptly and collect it in memory.*

Mistake #2. Thesis statement.

Incorrect: *There are several ideas which differentiate the modern youth community and teenagers of the past century.*

The thesis statement above is incomplete, as it does not show the initial topic of the essay. A proper thesis statement should present the subjects that will be compared and contrasted, and provide the critical idea on the comparison and the contrasting part. The reader should catch the main idea and concepts which are to be discussed in the following paper.

Correct: *A young community of the 21st century obtains many more opportunities in education, entertainment, leisure, and business deals, while teenagers of the past century* *had more restrictions on the mentioned issues and were limited in approaches of self-development.*

Mistake #3. Limited conclusion.

Incorrect: *In this essay, we have analyzed the peculiarities which differentiate modern youth from the ones living in the past century. We have identified the aspects of educational and leisure issues which occur in their everyday life.*

The example of the conclusion lacks essential information which would summarize the whole paper in one paragraph. Moreover, the first sentence of the conclusion is the inappropriately paraphrased thesis statement. An excellent summary should reveal the similarities and differences that you have found while researching these issues.

Correct: *On the whole, we have defined that modern youth have more chances to gain education at any university in the world and have opportunities to win the grant for free education overseas. Teenagers of the 20th century had some restrictions in educational programs and did not have chances to study abroad for free. Unlike the older generation of teenagers, these days, young people can travel, visit exhibitions, and attend courses.*

5.2. Argumentative Essay

An argumentative essay requires a student to analyze, investigate, conclude, and evaluate the arguments of the collected information. The most important part of this type of essay is to establish your position concerning the aspects that were revealed in it. You should support or refute the demonstrated issue based on some evidence.

Mistake #1. One general idea for each sentence.

Incorrect: *People often claim that children who live in a one-parent family usually suffer from emotional and physical disorders. Some scientists even conducted research on this issue and proved that there are many health and mental problems which occur for the child in such families. When we talk about parents, we might suppose that they have decided to* *live apart for their emotional balance. They have made a decision referring to their intimate problems.*

The example above shows two ideas in one paragraph. First, the writer explains how divorce influences the well being of the children, and afterward, he or she describes the reason for separation ("Argumentative Essays"). When you start the paragraph, put one idea in the first sentence and stick to it till the end. After you have finished with one purpose, move to the second in the next paragraph.

Correct: *People often claim that children, who live in a one-parent family, usually suffer from emotional and physical disorders. Some scientists even conducted research on this issue and proved that there are many health and mental problems which occur for the child in such families. As a result, children might obtain bad marks at school and become a problem child concerning behavior.*

However, we cannot suppose what would have happened if the parents continued to live together. Typically, parents decide to separate due to some personal conflicts which have been impacting the child's environment.

Mistake #2. Supporting evidence.

Incorrect: *Children in the one-parent family become very sensitive to the environment. They feel lack of attention from the mother or father and become isolated from the surroundings. As a result, children may commit suicide or follow the wrong path by becoming criminals.*

The example shows a new idea of the essay, but there is no evidence indicated to prove the idea ("Purdue OWL: Essay Writing"). An argumentative essay should be based on supporting evidence to inform the reader about real problems. You may research surveys or case studies which would contain the information about your idea.

Correct: *Children in the one-parent family become very sensitive to the environment. They feel lack of attention from the mother or father and become isolated from their surroundings. According to American police data, children who live in a one-parent family may commit* *suicide or follow the wrong path by becoming criminals. Psychologists who work with the police say that children do so to attract the attention of their parents.*

5.3. Narrative Essay

A narrative essay requires that the student should tell a story based on personal experience. Like any writing, it should include the introduction, main body, and the conclusion. The fundamental aspect of the structure is to organize each idea to attract the reader's attention and make your essay enjoyable to read.

Mistake #1. Introduction.

Incorrect: *During my first visit to the United States, I got the experience of living in the big city. I imagined so many opportunities for career and education. I was hoping to make plenty of friends from all over the world who would introduce me to their cultural peculiarities. I did not think of negative circumstances living in America and was determined to enjoy my stay there.*

The example introduction above seems to be completed at first glance. Nevertheless, each sentence is a separate part of the chain which does not catch the reader immediately. In a narrative essay, you should positively present your experience, starting from the first paragraph, even if the composition tells a sad story.

Correct: *When I got the chance to visit the United States of America, I became extremely excited about that news. It is true that there are plenty of opportunities for young people to become successful in career and education. Moreover, America is a multinational country, which means that I would be able to meet new people and discover their cultures. I had no idea how I would manage to live there, but I was optimistically determined to enjoy my stay there.*

In general, you should write an essay with vast diversity of descriptive adjectives if you present a life experience. Each paragraph should contain one idea which would be supported with the examples and circumstances that have led to that event. Moreover, you should also demonstrate your feelings and emotions, giving the opportunity for the reader to experience those events with you. Each event you demonstrate in your paper may also be supported by the circumstances before and after. When you present the post-event emotions, the reader may see how those particular life experiences have influenced you, whether negatively or positively. Additionally, you may provide the reader with some advice and recommendations to follows in similar situations.

5.4. Critical Essay

This type of writing requires a student to analyze the reading and present the critical points of it. The overuse of criticism in this kind of paper is considered to be inappropriate and usually leads to getting negative marks ("Critical Essay"). The critical essay should not include your emotional attitude to the reading. Moreover, while criticizing some issue within the materials, the student should support it with quotations to guarantee the understanding of the reader.

Mistake #1. Material analysis.

Incorrect: *There was a vigorously debated topic on whether the prisoners of Montblare should work. Some people claim that it is inappropriate to allow them to work in prison, while others insist that it is highly essential. It is a widespread stereotype that prisoners must stay in jail without being occupied by activities. By such inactivity, they would be able to surround themselves with the past events and feel guilt for the things they have done.*

The example above presents one idea about the scandal in Monblare prison. However, the writer has not mentioned any information from any material, survey sources, or debates concerning that issue. While writing a critical essay, you should provide the reader with the author's view, the central ideas of the reading, and show your understanding of the matter. As it was mentioned above, in order to support particular aspects of the reading, you should use quotations from the source.

Correct: *There was a vigorously debated topic on whether the prisoners of Montblare should work. Some people claim that it is inappropriate to allow them to work in prison, while others insist that it is highly essential. According to the findings which were discovered in the article, 77% of the prisoners in France are engaged in preferred activities* *during the sentence. Based on these results, we may suppose that prisoners who have been working in prison may enter the society after the prison term with some skills and knowledge obtained in prison.*

Mistake #2. Personal pronouns.

Incorrect: *The book that I have chosen for this particular writing is Plato's Apology. For me, the fundamental idea of this paper is how people limit themselves by being educated in only one field or subject. I have found one significant quotation of Socrates' dialogue which represents the central aspect of the whole book. "This man, on the one hand, believes that he knows something, while not knowing [anything]. On the other hand, I – equally ignorant – do not believe [that I know anything]." For me, this quote demonstrates that people consider themselves as wise while knowing nothing about wisdom.*

In general, the paragraph is written well according to the requirements for the critical essay. There is one fundamental idea which is proven with the quote from the book ("Critical Essay"). However, the writer applies too many personal pronouns which are not correct to use in this type of writing. Personal pronouns should only be used when there is a requirement to present your opinion on the particular topic.

Correct: *Plato's Apology is the book which remains central for critical writing. The key idea of this material is how people limit themselves by being educated in only one field or subject. There is one significant quotation of Socrates' dialogue which represents the central aspect of the whole book. "This man, on the one hand, believes that he knows something, while not knowing [anything]. On the other hand, I – equally ignorant – do not believe [that I know anything]." In general, this statement demonstrates that people consider themselves as wise while knowing nothing about wisdom.*

5.5. Definition Essay

The definition essay is aimed at explaining the particular term to the reader. The critical requirement of this type of writing is to maintain clear and precise language to deliver the explanation accurately ("Writing a Definition Essay: Outline, Format, Structure, Examples, Topics"). The definition and the description may be observed both from the one point and from the writer's viewpoint. The structure of the paper is simple, as it includes the analysis and explanation of the term concerning its function, components, and analysis.

Mistake #1. Incomplete introduction.

Incorrect: *The term is highly demanded to be explained in psychology. Scientists determine it as the driving force for humanity and that it establishes the individual's character. This essay is aimed at explaining the definition of the term as well as presenting its functioning.*

The example illustrates an entirely incomplete introduction as well as the absence of a proper thesis statement. First, the writer has not mentioned which term will be described in the essay. The writer provided us with the general information about it and the field of its functioning ("Writing a Definition Essay: Outline, Format, Structure, Examples, Topics"). Then, there are no specific details which would present us the background for writing this essay. Be sure to include the necessary information in your introduction and create the thesis statement according to the instructions. An appropriate thesis statement should reveal not only the key idea, but also present some issues which would inform the reader about the following essay.

Correct: *The term "humanness" is highly demanded as a subject of explanation and definition in psychology. Plenty of scientists determine it as the driving force for humanity and that it establishes the individual's character. The core components of this term are to maintain general qualities, such as kindness, love, patience, understanding, support, and dignity.*

In this part of the guide, we have determined common mistakes committed in the structure of essays. We hope these comprehensive recommendations will assist you while writing papers; you will do your best to avoid such mistakes. Good luck!

Works Cited

"Argumentative Essays." *Owl.English.Purdue.edu*, 2017.

https://owl.english.purdue.edu/owl/resource/685/05/.

"Compare & Contrast Essays." *Eapfoundation.com*, 2017.

http://www.eapfoundation.com/writing/essays/candc/.

"Critical Essay." *Essay-Writing-Tips.com*, 2017.

http://www.essay-writing-tips.com/types-of-essays/critical-essay.html.

"Writing a Definition Essay: Outline, Format, Structure, Examples, Topics." *Custom-Essays.org*,

2017. http://www.custom-essays.org/essay_types/Definition_Essay.html.

Chapter 6. Paraphrasing, Summarizing, Quoting

Academic writing is impossible to imagine without conducting research and collecting a database of knowledge on the topic. In order to ensure that your essay fits the requirements of sophisticated and advanced writing, you should take into account the methods of paraphrasing, summarizing, and quoting, and at the same time avoid plagiarism.

Differences Between Paraphrasing, Summarizing, and Quoting

The primary difference between the three terms refers to the format of the idea integration.

Paraphrasing means to use the concept from a text, but to convert it using your own words.

Summarizing is narrowing a larger amount of data into a specific idea.

Quoting means using the exact words of the author in the essay utilizing the correct formatting style mentioned later in this section.

All three types of writing tools have the same purpose to help a writer to:

- Enhance the arguments.

- Reference the original source being analyzed.

- Implement examples on the topic.

- Convey to the reader that the statements provided are objective.

- Illustrate the depth of the research conducted on the topic ("Purdue OWL: Quoting, Paraphrasing, and Summarizing").

Paraphrasing

Paraphrasing is a helpful tool to be used during the essay writing process. Paraphrasing means interpreting the passage from the original text in your own words. Usually, the paraphrased text is shorter than the original one and narrowed to the point without unnecessary background information ("Purdue OWL: Quoting, Paraphrasing, and Summarizing"). The tool is utilized to illustrate the essence in the form with a personal orientation on the one idea only ("Purdue OWL: Paraphrase Exercises").

* The citations in all the examples mentioned below are formatted according to MLA style.

Example #1:

Original Text	Incorrect Paraphrasing
"In the workplace, workers can have a low or high level of participation in decision-making about issues such as how to do the job, who does what job, what products are produced, who is employed, what wages are, how marketing is carried out and what investments are made. In an owner or management-dominated workplace, worker decision-making is highly restricted, perhaps limited to how to undertake an assigned task or when to take breaks" (Barker and Martin 6).	*In the working environment, laborers can have a low or abnormal engagement in making diverse decisions about issues: for example, how to carry out the occupation, who obtains a certain position at the department, what the salaries are, who is engaged in the working process, what compensations are, the means by which advertising is completed, and what ventures are produced. In a proprietor or administration-ruled working environment, the decision-making process made by an employee is exceedingly confined, maybe restricted to how to undertake a task or when to take breaks (Barker and Martin 6).*

The mentioned example is incorrect as the writer used the method of simply changing the key words into synonyms. It is worth mentioning that to paraphrase means to find the initial idea and convert it in a way to make the reader comprehend the narrowed sense of the selected text. While paraphrasing, try to change the structure of the sentences. You may make the sentences shorter or longer, combine them, or split them ("Avoiding Plagiarism: Quoting and Paraphrasing"). You may omit some words or substitute them with synonyms.

Original Text	Correct Paraphrasing
"In the workplace, workers can have a low or high level of participation in decision-making about issues such as how to do the job, who does what job, what products are produced, who is employed, what wages are, how marketing is carried out and what investments are made. In an owner or management-dominated workplace, worker decision-making is highly restricted, perhaps limited to how to undertake an assigned task or when to take breaks" (Barker and Martin 6).	*In the working environment, employees mainly perform the provided tasks rather than participate in work and wage division, deciding which products to manufacture, or implementing the marketing campaign. The decision-making process is carried out by the owners or managers as their primary responsibility (Barker and Martin 5-6).*

Example #2:

Original Text	Incorrect Paraphrasing
"The arguments for a 'female advantage' in leadership generally stem from the belief that women are more likely than men to adopt collaborative and empowering leadership	*From the leadership perspective, females are considered to utilize a more collaborative approach than males, who prefer a more "command-and-control" style.*

styles, while men are disadvantaged because their leadership styles include more command-and-control behaviors and the assertion of power" (Paustian-Underdahl, Walker and Woehr 1129).	

The main mistake of the paraphrased sentence above is the absence of the citation. If you forget to insert a source for the idea taken, it is regarded as plagiarism. Notice that even a well-paraphrased part of the text is considered to be stolen if you do not mention the author.

You may read more detailed data on how to cite correctly further in the book.

Original Text	Correct Paraphrasing
"The arguments for a 'female advantage' in leadership generally stem from the belief that women are more likely than men to adopt collaborative and empowering leadership styles, while men are disadvantaged because their leadership styles include more command-and-control behaviors and the assertion of power" (Paustian-Underdahl, Walker and Woehr 1129).	*From the leadership perspective, females are considered to utilize a more collaborative approach than males, who prefer a more "command-and-control" style (Paustian-Underdahl, Walker and Woehr 1129).*

Summarizing

Summarizing may be explained as the interpretation of the author's statements in your own words. A summary of a particular text abstract is usually much shorter than the original part, as the writer is picking up the information and conveying the general idea ("Quoting, Summarizing, and Paraphrasing").

Example #1:

Original Text	Incorrect Summarizing
"Lotteries are by far the most popular games of chance, both in terms of participation frequency and expenditure. Moreover, lotteries are highly relevant to fiscal revenue and redistribution. They generate substantial regressive tax revenue as low-income players spend a higher proportion of their income on lotteries. Most studies that have addressed this question make use of individualistic explanations and focus on cognitive biases" (Beckert and Lutter 1167).	Lotteries may be reviewed as one of the most widespread forms of recreational chance taking, which takes into account participation frequency. The popularity of this type of game impacts a variety of economic issues. The initial problem concerns income expenses for the lottery among low-income inhabitants. As well, according to numerous studies, the problem may be of an idealistic nature and arising from cognitive prejudices.

The main problem illustrated in the example is the size of the summarized part. The example mentioned above is more similar to paraphrasing as it suits the size of the original text. Summarizing relates to taking the idea and covering it in one or two sentences.

Original Text	Correct Summarizing
"Lotteries are by far the most popular games of chance, both in terms of participation frequency and expenditure. Moreover, lotteries are highly relevant to fiscal revenue and redistribution. They generate substantial regressive tax revenue as low-income players spend a higher proportion of their income on lotteries. Most studies that have addressed	Lotteries impact a variety of economic issues, as the initial problem concerns income expenses for the lottery among low-income inhabitants. This is considered to be of an idealistic nature and from cognitive prejudices (Beckert and Lutter 1167).

this question make use of individualistic explanations and focus on cognitive biases" (Beckert and Lutter 1167).	

Example #2:

Original Text	Incorrect Summarizing
"As Sam Walton grew up he was always an ambitious boy. He attended Hickman High School in Columbia where he played basketball and football, in which he was the starting quarterback for the football team and led them to the state title in 1935. Besides being athletic he was also a political figure at school, too" (Ghosh 4).	*Sam Walton attended Hickman High School in Columbia where he was a basketball and football player, being a very athletic boy (Ghosh 4).*

The example shows that the primary and most significant points are not highlighted. The summary concerns underlining the essential points and inserting them into one or a couple of sentences. In order to efficiently summarize the data, you should decide on what the target of the sentence is and what information is primary for being recognized by the reader.

Original Text	Correct Summarizing
"As Sam Walton grew up he was always an ambitious boy. He attended Hickman High School in Columbia where he played basketball and football, in which he was the starting quarterback for the football team and led them to the state title in 1935. Besides	*Sam Walton grew up as a very ambitious boy, as during his studies at Hickman High School in Columbia, he showed his team-playing abilities leading the football team to the state title (Ghosh 4).*

being athletic he was also a political figure at school, too" (Ghosh 4).	

Quoting

Quoting is one of the most valuable tools while writing an essay, as it helps to enhance the arguments with statements taken from academic sources. This means using the exact words of the author without any changes. You do not need to think of ways of making it different, as the only thing you have to do is find the relevant quotation, copy and paste it, and cite the author.

Example #1:

Incorrect Quoting
"Obviously Shirley Jackson was ahead of her time" (Mohammadi, Rezvan and Heidarian 219).

Many students insert quotations to fit the word count rather than the actual context, which is the most widespread problem. Generalized phrases, as well as well-known facts, are not to be quoted. Find specific information and cite the most valuable part of it to support your arguments.

Correct Quoting
"The author shows that she is hopeful of changing the baseless superstitions by the new generation" (Mohammadi, Rezvan and Heidarian 219).

Example #2:

Incorrect Quoting
According to Hoyt, "racism - (original definition) is the belief that all members of a purported race possess characteristics, abilities, or qualities specific to that race, especially so as to distinguish it as inferior or superior to another race or other races."

Any quotation requires proper citing and formatting in order to avoid plagiarism. The mistake of the mentioned example is the absence of the page number from where the statement was taken.

Correct Quoting (Option 1)
According to Hoyt, "racism - (original definition) is the belief that all members of a purported race possess characteristics, abilities, or qualities specific to that race, especially so as to distinguish it as inferior or superior to another race or other races" (225).
Correct Quoting (Option 2)
"Racism - (original definition) is the belief that all members of a purported race possess characteristics, abilities, or qualities specific to that race, especially so as to distinguish it as inferior or superior to another race or other races" (Hoyt 225).

In case you selected a quotation consisting of more than four lines (a block quote) it requires specific formatting as well:

Correct Quoting
According to Hoyt: *Those who advocate a precising definition of racism argue that racism should not be considered a merely psychological or cognitive phenomenon, but that, instead, it should be conceived as an action committed against its victims, and that to commit the action of racism, one must have access to the power required to inflict racist harm of the sort that promotes and preserves the status and privileges of the dominant social group and the subordination of the nondominant social group (225).*

The vital issue is to find correct sources which fit the topic and are helpful enough for your essay. Integrating ideas from academic sources is the point which makes an essay look well-constructed. Using the hints on paraphrasing, summarizing, and quoting illustrated above will make the writing process easy, and your essay will be complete and free of plagiarism. Good luck!

Works Cited

"Avoiding Plagiarism: Quoting and Paraphrasing." *Writing.Wisc.edu*, 2017.

   https://writing.wisc.edu/Handbook/QPA_paraphrase2.html.

Barker, Chris, and Brian Martin. "Participation: The Happiness Connection." *Journal Of Public*

   Deliberation, vol 7, no. 1, 2011, pp. 5-6.

Beckert, Jens, and Mark Lutter. "Why the Poor Play the Lottery: Sociological Approaches to

   Explaining Class-Based Lottery Play." *Sociology*, vol 47, no. 6, 2012, p. 1167. *SAGE*

   Publications, doi:10.1177/0038038512457854.

Ghosh, Koustab. "Sam Walton: The Exemplary Retail Leader (Case Study)." *AFBE Journal*, vol 7,

   no. 1, 2014, p. 4.

Hoyt, C. "The Pedagogy of the Meaning of Racism: Reconciling a Discordant Discourse." *Social*

   Work, vol 57, no. 3, 2012, p. 225. *Oxford University Press (OUP)*, doi:10.1093/sw/sws009.

Mohammadi, Fatemeh Aziz et al. "Tradition and Modernity in Shirley Jackson's Lottery." *Research*

   Journal of English Language and Literature (RJELAL), vol 2, no. 3, 2017, p. 219.

Paustian-Underdahl, Samantha C. et al. "Gender and Perceptions of Leadership Effectiveness: A

   Meta-Analysis of Contextual Moderators." *Journal of Applied Psychology*, vol 99, no. 6,

   2014, pp. 1129-1145. doi:10.1037/a0036751.

"Purdue OWL: Paraphrase Exercises." *Owl.English.Purdue.edu*, 2017.

   https://owl.english.purdue.edu/owl/resource/619/1/.

"Purdue OWL: Quoting, Paraphrasing, and Summarizing." *Owl.English.Purdue.edu*, 2017.

   https://owl.english.purdue.edu/owl/resource/563/01/.

"Quoting, Summarizing, and Paraphrasing." *Web.Williams.edu*, 2017.

Final Thoughts

Hopefully, this book will serve you as a devoted companion for years. It should be mentioned that there is no book in the world that would help you avoid all mistakes. On the bright side, the amount of mistakes you make will decrease provided that you follow all of our recommendations.

Most students are incredibly busy and unable to read such a long book each time an essay is to be written. Therefore, we recommend you read it from time to time when you have free time and make notes about mistakes that are the most common for you. Also, you should return to *Essay Writing Police: On Guard of Your Literacy* in case you need to complete something very important, such as a scholarship essay.

If you need more help with academic writing, you should also refer to other books from the EssayShark series. There's always room for perfection — remember that. Now, we wish you good luck in studying and bid farewell for some short time.

Made in the USA
Middletown, DE
26 April 2018